NOT BY BREAD ALONE

NOT BY BREAD ALONE

THE THOUSAND YEARS OF THE FRENCH REVOLUTION

DOUGLAS BULLIS

GIBBS·SMITH PUBLISHER

PEREGRINE SMITH BOOKS
SALT LAKE CITY

This is a Peregrine Smith Book, published by
Gibbs Smith, Publisher, P.O. Box 667, Layton,
Utah 84041

Design by J. Scott Knudsen

Manufactured in the United States of America

**Library of Congress Cataloging-in-
Publication Data**

Bullis, Douglas.
    Not by bread alone : the thousand years of the
French Revolution/Douglas Bullis.
        p.   cm.
    ISBN 0-87905-345-3
    1. France–History–Fiction. 2. Peasantry–
France–History–Fiction. I. Title.
PS3552.U453N6   1989
813'.54–dc20   89–36422
                                               CIP

The paper used in this publication meets the minimum requirement of American National Standard
of Information Sciences–Permanence of Paper for
Printed Library Materials, ANSI Z39.48–1984 ∞

To Frank Gorin, for seeing this in a pile of neglected papers.

And to Andrew Madar, who at the age of fourteen already knows history is of this.

Contents

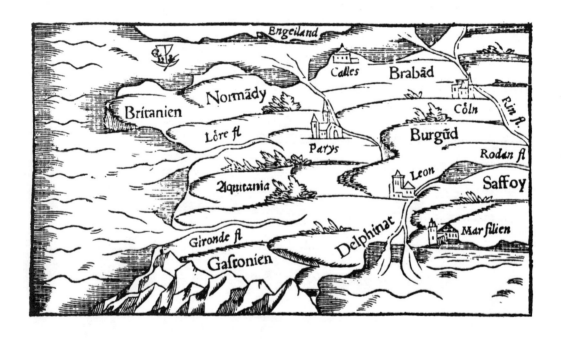

1003
After the Thousandth Year

The moods of the Mediterranean had been the moods of things opposite: sun/soil, night/day, sweetness and pain and the unmingling of time's things. It was a universe of pieces in which everything could be found.

But sea peoples and northmen knew of mist and lost sun, the blendings of the sea at once giving and taking. They knew the heat that is haze and the clouds that bring rain, the blue and gray land made of illusions, the houses of neighbors becoming distance-thin daubs, the vessel rounding the point in the brushed sun's glaze indistinguishable between a husband's return and a pirate sliding inland to plunder. A knowledge of mists knows the sea One.

· · · · • · · · ·

The family came to the place where the local lord had granted them the use of a spring. They would live there for the rest of their lives, so they brought oxen, wagons, axes, knives, chickens, children, dogs. They made shacks for themselves, saving the hearts of the trees for the timbers of the church, keeping for themselves only the limbs, twigs, leaves. The children kept the fires going, the women foraged and cooked, and the men cut the stone and carved it. When it was winter they threw the stones into the fires then cut them when they were warm.

The water there was sound's perfume—eddies, slow places, flow without rhythm, swiftnesses beyond the ear's power. The spring was everything the sea would one day be. Flowing its own way, thief of good soil, its nestling was so soft that it alone could move mountains. Whatever water was, they knew the earth could be broken by its being.

Hence they used its trickle well. They turned the spring aside to pool in an empty field. That drained the soil where they wanted to build. Then the water broke into remnant stones too big for oxen but not for fire.

A pit was dug beneath a boulder as far as it could go. A fire was built in it, first limbs and then logs, building the heat until the bottom of the boulder was dull red and the top hissed steam when water was flicked on. Then the coals were buried, the soil tamped hard, and bucket after bucket of water was brought from the spring and trickled over the stone's top until with no warning there was a deep snap and a cloud of ashes and steam hissed high. Then they cheered and the oxen took away the pieces for the foundation of their church.

For the millennium year of 1000 had come and gone and the world hadn't ended. Every sign in the books and the stars had said the end was near. But perhaps they hadn't been prepared. Perhaps they had learned only to avoid sin, not how to love. So the water of life gave them the power to go on, and eyes that had closed last night to dread now opened to hope. From the tellers of the time there came these words:

> So on the threshold of the aforesaid Thousandth Year, some two or three years after it, it befell them all, especially in Italy and Gaul, that the fabric of the world was rebuilt. Every nation rivaled the other which should worship in the seemliest house. It was as though the world had shaken off her old robes and was clothing herself everywhere in garments of white churches.

The priests told them the shape they wanted built, a shape they had learned from a forgotten conquerer, so they called it *roman*. And they knew the direction they wanted the building to face: east, toward Jerusalem, so that every step toward the altar was a step closer to God.

10

But the rest had to be learned: how to harden crude iron into chisels by heating it and pounding it and quenching it sizzling in buckets of water, and doing this over and over again until the metal rang when it struck the stone. How to break the stone loose from its cliff by driving wooden stakes into the cracks and then flooding them with water until the wood swelled and the rock groaned and the stone split free. How to design the cuts of the pieces using fingers and water on a chalk-dusted table. How to hold lines up with circles so that the roof became like a barrel turned inside out, not clenched but thrust. How to arc stone across space by cutting it into shapes that would pinch themselves so tightly that once the trestle was removed, even if the rest of the structure would someday fall, the part that would remain was also the most delicate.

They began with oaks, and of those, only trees three hundred or more years old, thicker around than the village's oldest ox, whose heartwood was so dense it could bear almost any load. They cut off the outer wood while the tree was still standing, then left it to weather a year. They used the soft layers for shingles and the bark to tan leather.

Then they cut the trees down and squared the limbs and trunks with adzes. Oxen dragged the pieces to a stream that had been dammed into a pond. The beams soaked there ten years, weighted with heavy stones so the water could take its own time in carrying away the sap. Then the beams were dragged out and lifted onto trestles in sheds so air could reach them on all sides. There they dried another ten years.

The men who raised the beams took the same care. No beam was left unexposed to the air, so that even in wet times it would have a place where dampness could escape. Nails of bent iron would molder away their strength but dovetails would not, so every timber reflected the geometry through which the carpenter preserved the life of his world.

Because the family had cleared the land around this church, the local lord allowed them to farm it under his protection in fief, in satisfaction of the words of the lawyers of the time, that no land or man should be without a lord. When the family was later confirmed in the church by the lord's bishop, the lord shunned the observance so they could not plead of him to adopt his name. They therefore took unto themselves the name of the fief itself, to last as long as the family should live.

There the Lefiefs began.

1003: AFTER THE THOUSANDTH YEAR

1193

The Return of Gonbault's Lefief's Son

September's quick storms wither into the first week of October. Then come the thick morning fogs and the bright afternoons of Saint Martin's Summer. In the five weeks between the first storm-broken twigs and the somber jaggedness of All Saints' Day, the harvest is embraced.

The time of the wheat and apples and grapes now long done, this is the time of the gifts of the earth, the gifts not tended by the hand of man. They are gathered from the wildnesses that surround every hamlet and field. First the walnuts scattered on the ground in their decaying husks—nutmeats for feasts and dyestuff from the husks to blacken winter's clothes. Draped broken branches across doorways to keep out flies. Children groan at the order to gather acorns, tedious work but food for the winter sows to keep their flesh pink. And to make sweet pies with acorn-flour crust filled with cream and wild berries.

Lords' falconers haunt the field edges and bogs, unhooding their birds and shooing them with yelps to flush pheasants, quail, partridge, ducks. Eel hunters poise along the swamp rims, cocking their spears and holding tightly to the woven hemp twines that retrieve them. Mushrooms poke out of the wet leaves and damp stumps. In the woods sudden yells and furious barking announce that hunters are lunging pikes at a cornered boar, squealing and pawing with rage. Dogs lie whimpering in their spilled bowels until the boar is dead. Then the men come over to the dogs and pat them and talk to them in low voices and end them.

The pale green leaves of streamside poplars crinkle to yellow, next spring's young buds pushing them until they snap away into the wind. Though the sun glitters brightly on top of the water, underneath it is murky and dull as the summer's end slips toward the sea. A leaf is caught, spun, dragged into an eddy to vanish forever. *Twrrts* come from the stream-edge birds, *zzdzs* from the crickets. Wrens flit through the blackberry briars, cleaning the last ants from the thorns. October's wing shapes reveal the forms of their flight, from the tireless taut bulk of the upthrusting young duck to the rapier-bent tension of the landgull's long glide. The soil, released at last from the management of the plow, crumbles into furrows filling with fallen seeds. Insect clouds, much diminished by the rains, tremble in the coppery sun of late day. And everywhere autumn smells: wet moss, pine, mud, stagnant water, souring manure, burning weeds, wild garlic, dill.

Then the mood of the weather changes, robbing the afternoon to pay for the morning, twisting its cold roots deeper into the soil. As the summer was of flesh, October is of bone. Men gather in fire-lighted caves, elbow to elbow, breath steaming despite the roaring fire, tasting the harvest's new wine, sniffing through its mustiness, then quaffing it deeply from carved wooden mugs. The smell of the embers as they are snuffed out. The ache of the fall.

Slaughter. Short, grim knifework, spilling the year's blood as animals bellow and flare their eyes and struggle against the ropes binding their hooves. Quick knives, sure knives, splitting the bellies and scraping off the hides and cutting hazelwood spits to skewer the meats. Hides are gathered into thick, nauseating bundles, to be taken to the tannery. Then comes the division. The smith gets the head of the largest cow and pig, and after his wife has boiled them down to the last sinew for soup, he'll nail the skulls up alongside his dozens of others, an advertisement for his shop and how many seasons he's been there. Women will mince the sweetbreads and delicacies for sprouty, a hot pie made with vegetable sprouts and nuts and sorb berries. The sheep will be spared, for they have fat and thick fleece to keep them alive through the snows until the first parsley-spring of February.

Then comes a reverential silence as the local *seigneur* comes to claim his Lord's Haunch, the best piece of meat from each man's cows and pigs, and his *dime*, a tenth of the chestnuts and smoked sausages, eels, leeks. The people fill his barrels with the new wine and he sips a cup with them before going off on his horse. Next comes the *cure* with his two black kettles, one of them nine times the size of the other. When they are both filled, he takes the smaller for himself and marks on his tally whose tithe is done. After his due has been loaded onto a mule, the women present him with sausages of boiled chicken mortared into a paste with fresh cress, then stuffed into scraped gut. One of the women gives him a basket of hard-boiled goose eggs for the traditional priest's breakfast after the last mass each Sunday in December.

When the division is done, the silence breaks. Backs are slapped, old women are kissed, children are let free for the day. Everyone is giddy, looking forward to the feast. So the bitterest work of the year, meat salting, passes swiftly, rhythmed on through by the catchtags of songs. The frost is an agony, but they must work with bare fingers as they slice the meat thin and rub salt into its fibers. They warm themselves often with huge gulps of wine from half-warm barrels stacked next to the fires. The beef is sliced into slivers and dried in the cold night air. Tripes and soft parts are half-cooked by boiling, mixed with fat and blood, then rolled into the sausages they'll fry every morning through the rest of the winter. Bacons and hams are salted and trussed up in sacks, then punctured with tiny slits and soaked in barrels of brine before smoking.

Plumes of smoke from hardwood fires smear the horizon as the smokehouses finish the last task of the year. Then it's over. One harvest in six is a total ruin, two or more yield less than they could, two others are so-so, and then there's one, just one, with an ending like this. November comes with cold that clenches like a snake around a rat.

Gonbault Lefief ventures out into the mist to set a snare for a crow. In the distance he sees a figure walking toward him through Noyers, the walnut tree place. With eyes growing weak at the age of thirty-nine, Gonbault does not recognize the figure as his son, Josseret.

And Josseret does not recognize him. Barely twenty-three, he trudges with a limp, one foot severed of its toes by the scimitar of a Moslem. His eyes, too, are weak, although he can see enough to recognize the shapes of the old buildings,

17

the trees he climbed for nuts as a child, the pasture now empty after the slaughter. The backs of both hands and his cheeks are disfigured from a flood of flaming oil that found its way through the seams of a leather tent covering the ladder he and twenty other men were using to scale a parapet in Syria. Josseret was lucky. He had time enough to shield his eyes with his hands. The hot fumes merely weakened his sight and burnt him. Others were blinded or suffocated when they inhaled the burning liquid. Of the fifty-odd men between fifteen and twenty who began the Crusade from the church in the center of the hamlet, only Josseret has returned, in a body so exhausted it will carry him but scarce another year.

But the stories he will tell! Of steel so honed it could cut a falling cloth by the cloth's mere weight alone! Of immense domed roofs held up by the merest whisper of windowed stone walls! Of tableware so lustrous and thin one can see the shadow of a hand through it! Of forked instruments that can move even the smallest morsel of food to the mouth! Of lapis, of onyx, of ruby, and painted jars more spendid than these jewels! Of spices that turn the muddy stink of raw meat into odors of flowers so delicate they must surely be the food of angels fallen to earth! Of sallow men who have no lust for women (Oh, how Beric the village priest will despise the laughs *that* story will bring!). Of things with names no one here has ever experienced – orange, lemon, sugar, syrup, sherbet, julep, elixir, jar, mattress, sofa, muslin, satin, fustian, bazaar, caravan, tariff, traffic, sloop, barge, cable, guitar, lute, tambourine, zenith, alembic, almanac! And above all, a poem he heard from a brothel woman as she disrobed for him:

From the moment you were brought into the world
A ladder was before you that you might escape.
First you were mineral,
Later a plant,
Then you became animal,
Afterward a man.
When you travel next,

18

You will be an angel.
But pass on even then, beyond angelhood
And enter the ocean of God.
Leave aside your Son of God
And be One of God,
For God is great.

Gonbault, his son still a village and a field away, is intent on the crow he has just snared. He strangles the frantic bird with his bare hands, then hangs it on a cord to rot from the limb of a tree in the middle of his field, the first scarecrow for next spring.

1260

The Consecration

The inhabitants of Chartres have combined to aid in the building of their church by transporting the stones themselves. They have formed associations, some of guildsmen and others of merchants, and have admitted no one to their company unless they had been to confession, renounced their feuds, and forgiven their debtors. This done, they elect a chief under whose direction they take up the ropes to their wagons. Who has ever heard of such a thing? Princes, merchants, townsmen—all have bent their backs to the harnesses of wagons like animals. And while they drew them, so heavy from the quarries that often more than a thousand were attached to one wagon, they marched in such silence that not one murmur was heard. If one did not see them, one would not know they were there. When they halt on the road, nothing is heard but the sounds of salvation. The priests who preside over each wagon exhort every one to acceptance of fault and resolution to better their lives. One sees old people, young children, parents, grandfathers, calling upon God with words of glory and praise. When they reach the place of the church they arrange the wagons in a spiritual encampment. During the whole night they celebrate the watch with canticles and hymns. On each wagon they light candles and lamps, and there they place the sick among them and bring them the water of life and the precious relics of God for relief. Nothing like it has ever before been seen.

21

· · · · · · · · ·

The Consecration was to be on the Feast of the Annunciation. Everyone knew that generations before even the half-century was decided. The day the virgin girl accepted into her womb the salvation of mankind. It could not be on any other day.

They knew about God the Father, they knew the face. They would see that face someday, they didn't want to see it now. And they knew about God the Son, preacher, dreamer, lifter of men, who falls in love with the idea of love and cries at the end, Why have you forsaken me?

There were feast days to those two beings, judgment and promise, but in all the worship given to them, a prayer of hope was not included.

The frightened girl listened in disbelief as the angel said, "*Ave, Maria. Ave Maria Stellis*. The Lord is with you," and she wondered, How can that be? I am a virgin. But then she felt the first stirrings and she knew.

Their great-great-grandfathers had sung those words, *Ave Maria Stellis*, in the long cold night as they prayed beneath the wagons that groaned with stone. In the yellow flickering light of the fires they did not see or feel their rope-torn hands or bleeding feet. They felt only hope. And they sang those words as they planed the earth flat and began to set stone upon stone until there was a foundation so thick they knew it would never crack. The quarriers sang those words as they drove green wood wedges into the rocks' cracks and poured water over them until the wood swelled and the stone split free into slabs they then cubed and dressed with patterns of rough slits. The stonecutters sang them as they inscribed their geometries of candle wax and chalk mark, then hewed the columns and piers, pediments, buttresses, walls, their chisels singing with them as the stone fragments flew halfway across the shed. The stonecarvers sang those words, softly now, humming as lightly as their furrowing tools, shaping delicate faces, angels with trumpets, flowing beards of patriarchs, the stone sneers of gargoyles spitting water onto the parvis far far below.

And the poorest of all sang them lustily, bellowing Mary's praises as they devoted to her their only God-given gift: feet. Their roisterous hymn rose high from the pillartop where they worked, walking inside the spokes of their circular cage, the rotating drum twice their height, their hands braced against its spindle as they walked and walked, the drum rotating around them as the rope coiled around it descended to the parvis and grasped the net holding a gigantic planed slab cut to the shape of the new pier next to their own, so massive a stone a dozen of them could stand atop it. Then the song became a groan as they turned and trod the circle again in the other direction, until the drum had turned to take up the slack, lift, and pinion around, until the new stone was levered into place and the chocks fixed and the net slipped out from the gap between the new piece and the pier on which it would now settle forever.

And they cried the words as they knelt by the body with the blood flowing from its nose and the broken eyes and sunken ribs as the priest came running with the Host and Oil, running out of breath, running and still too late, running into the shadow of the pillar so high above.

Ave Maria Stellis, Star of the Sea.

It was the gray earth that gave this paradise its hues. From places they could hardly pronounce, the soils came. Boxes of malachite, sacks of lazuli, saddlebags of opal, agate, onyx, crystal. Sands from Turchestan that melted into deep green, cinnabar from Spain speckled with quicksilver, mysterious stones from Candia, that great rock fish rising from the sea, whose pounded dust makes glass blue. Scrapings from Abyssinia and Cyprus and Syria, brought in lead boxes on donkeys, camels, ships, caravans, and on the backs of pilgrims returning from the Holy Land. Boxes carried up to the altar to be placed beneath the statue of the Virgin and given to Her church.

And when the lead seal was broken and the lid spread back, the note folded inside the reddish dust was in a strange script the pilgrim said was Syriac, which he translated brokenly for the glassmakers:

Take thyself a fine slab of porphyry stone and a small quantity of clear water, then take thyself up a small portion of this color and slowly begin to crush it in a thumbnail's measure of the water. The period of a quarter part of the day is the least you must work it, but know you that you may grind

23

it for a week and the color will only become better. When this is finished to your satisfaction, take a thin wooden blade and gather the color nicely into a pot, but assure you that the pot is not of the stone that containeth the shells of old fishes, for that taints the color and makes it unseemly. With this preparation you may make flesh colors. Know you that first you must begin with a measure of lead white. Put it just as it is, without breaking it, into a pot of copper and place this over a fire until the lead white hath all turned to yellow. Then grind it and mix it with some of the color as you have prepared above. It will turn vermilion as you do, until the color is as that of flesh. If it be that you wish lighter faces, such as the child a-crib or women who have used powders, add a little more of the lead white, plus a little of green jasper. If it is that you wish faces more red, as from the wind or sun, add more of this vermilion. The colors that you see will be stronger somewhat after they have been heated. The longer the glass remains melted, the darker the colors will be. Yet be you careful not to take the heat away too quickly, for the glass will then splinter along the lines of its bubbles. Know you that the mosaics of Constantinople use thus this earth.

But the glassmakers did not sing as they stood at their tables. Around them were the boxes full of colored shards, cooled at last from the furnaces before which they had sweated as they peered past the waves of searing heat to the color pooling out of the lumpen earths beyond; and the boxes lined with long strips of tin they had melted and poured into finger-traced furrows along lengths of clean sand. And piled up around them were the finished carved webs of the giant rose windows that now they had to illumine with majesty.

Instead they spoke quietly. They were artisans, they knew their place. That place was found on the first page of nearly every illuminated manuscript, peering out from the lacework of the first letter. They could paint themselves there, into the decoration and fantasy, the happy artificier amid the writhing shapes and curling fluidities that streamed out to every corner of the world of invention and delight.

And they spoke of principles: Luminosity is majesty. The variety of colors reveals the variety of God's works. The colors of the border repeat those of the center, but only in fragments so they support, not rival, the theme. And one color alone is the uniting radiance by which all others receive their value: that color is blue.

. . . .

Then they knew the half-century in which it would happen, then the decade, then the year. The town normally counted as its population seven or eight thousand, not counting the women, bastards, and children, or the serfs who had not yet lived out their year and a day until they could call themselves free. And they knew who would be coming: three patriarchs, twelve cardinals, fifteen archbishops, eighty bishops, hundreds of abbots, chancellors of universities, doctors of theology, kings, princes, nobles, thousands of priests, and an unguessable number of ladies, pages, servants, horsetenders, trumpeters, esquires, knights, ambassadors, daughters, viscounts, clerks, physicians, blessed-medal stampers, candle dippers, stable sweepers, scullery boys, waiters, minstrels, jugglers, prostitutes, dung collectors, cutpurses, beggars, thieves. Every one of them wanted to be in the parvis on the Feast of the Annunciation.

Breadbaker Josquin Lefief rises first, before the dawn that begins the Day of the Feast. Accustomed to the upside-down life of the baker, he yawns, coughs, touches a pine splinter to the embers and strides through the corridor in the yellow flickerings of its light. He touches it to the shavings of the oven's fire pit—not the fire for baking yet, that won't be until dawn. But the fire to be warm by, and to see. He awakens the apprentices, lets them run their fingers through their hair, then gets them into their tunics. They drag sacks of flour out into the room while the oldest, almost a journeyman now, fills buckets of water from the well. Then before the work begins he gives them each a large mug of wine, with some bread and fresh cheese.

They begin. The apprentices pour the water slowly into the white dust and the journeyman blends it with his fingers until the mass begins to congeal into a dough of damp streakinesses. Then he adds yeast and more water as they continue stirring until the ball holds his fist's punch and is right.

Then bells. *Bells!* Bells from all over the town, a predawn polyphony rising to the moon, so tumultuous and strange it raises a set of dog howls as tone-matched as its peals.

Thin bells from far chapels, out on the edge of hearing, where the assembled peasants have been sleeping next to the warmth of their animals, and where they now rise and cross themselves and begin to sing *Ave Maria Stellis*.

Bells from the tent towns of the visiting monks, oilcloth abbeys complete with kitchens and cloisters vaulted with rope arched upon wood. And they, whose day perpetually begins at first light, rise as they always do, from their pallets, fully clothed in their habits, sliding into their slippers as they take up their candles and shuffle their way between the tentpegs and puddles to the gloomy chapel bordering the north side of their tent and begin to sing *Ave Maria Stellis*.

Bells from the townhouses, bold bongs to timid tinkles, awakening them to rooms with scented apple or pearwood fires, or to rooms crumbling with damp but which contain a fresh bed of new straw for Her. Kneeling on padded velvet cushions or plain wooden benches, before perspectiveless painted pictures or crude wooden carvings, and all of them singing *Ave Maria Stellis*.

Josquin and his apprentices now work steadily, silent except for *Ave*s, shaping the hundreds of loaves. Some long, some flat, some round, some knotted into pretzels to be carried through the streets on a hooked stick. Then come the whispers of the dawn, the dark passages of birds still too hungry to sing.

Now they build the fire up, piling on scrap wood still sappy and clutching its bark. Building it hot, roaring, sending up its yellow heat into the dome until the stones on the bottom are searing and right. Then! Out with the ashes! Quick lads! Out with them! She's hot! It's time!

Apprentices fly as they spade out the coals and Josquin drops in the stone plug to keep the shimmering heat in the dome. In goes a basin of water to make the crust crisp. Then! Off with the oilcloths! Sprinkle flour onto the paddle! Quick! Out of the pans and onto the paddle! It's double the number and today is *today*! Quick! Quick! *Quick!*

He is a rhythm of his life's experience as he handles the paddle. The journeyman turns the loaves three at a time onto the paddle as Josquin smooths them with a stroke of his thumb and forefinger, then darts out of the way as in comes an apprentice with a razor to cut angled slits across the top so they'll unfold as they bake. Josquin slides them into the far corner of the oven where they slip lumpily from the paddle and immediately begin to swell. Loaves, slits, paddle; loaves slits paddle, loaves, slits, paddle loavesslitspaddle, as the rush becomes a blur and they suck in their breath as they hear the water in the basin begin to sizzle and then steam, and then they go still faster. Every loaf must be in when the pan boils, so the oven can be closed and the steam left to do its work and when the bread comes out it'll cool so quickly they'll crackle like fire and the hardest part of the day will then be over and they'll cheer as the first one comes out and when its crust hits the cool air it will craze into a thousand steaming flakes and smell like heaven itself. *Ave!* Josquin cries. *Ave!* shouts the journeyman. *Ave!* yell the apprentices.

Then they are done. The stone falls away with the pry of a stick and Josquin takes out one small round loaf near the front and Yes! That's right! Listen to it! It finishes its crackling and someone gives him a clap on the back and he wipes his forehead and officially promotes the journeyman and gives all of them thumbs-up and they laugh and begin to sing *Ave Maria Stellis.*

· · · · · · · · ·

The beggars and cripples are the first ones to the parvis. It is their day above all, for She has known suffering and She knows succor. They have the privilege before prelates and princes to pass through the unopened door. And they come. Hunching along on wooden forearms strapped to their stumps, scraping up the steps on cradles holding what's left of their legs. Legs bent from a bad birth or broken on justice's wheel or lost among the screaming horses as the princes turned and rode through their midst leaving them to face the army beyond a galloping wall of swords and spearpoints and horses' flaring nostrils.

Across the townscape of fresh whitewash and roofs, the finest clothes are lifted from cabinets and chests, clothes now deeply scented with the potpourri in the backs of the drawers, the pot of fermenting verbena and lavender and rose, gathered just as the dew was ending so they wouldn't rot and wouldn't get dry, then layered with salt and left to ferment until the scent was perfect. Finally put into jars in the back of the drawers, behind the clothes made for this occasion alone. Robes, capes, chemises, velvets. Fustians, brocatelles, frisadues, kerseys. Satins, silks, lockrams, damasks. Cloth wefted of gold and warped of silk, then dyed in the saffron's yellow, the bedstraw's crimson, the woad's blue-white that colors a robe Her blue, the blue of the glass rose, the blue of water under a blue sky plied by the Ship of Jerusalem.

Clothes lifted from the neat folds into which they had only last night been pressed, now to be pressed again. Sprinkled, smoothed, scattered with jonquil, then creased again with heated smooth stones, the scent rising so warmly it will still be there long after the last crease has worn thin. Gold figured in blue, satin edged with damask, blue cloth brilliant in its hue. Seashell sequins, black velvets for widows, yellow tissue lined with lace, gray satin with peacock feathers and eyes, mantles, fur collars, ribbon wristlets. Even in the poorest house there is somewhere a ribbon of bright blue. Mary would understand these things. They would bring frowns from Father or Son. But it was Mary who gave birth to the child and knew how the child dreams and delights in the vivid and the bright and the free.

The streets are now alive with activity amid silence. By unspoken understanding no ordinary voice will be heard until the Consecration is over. The voice may sing. It may hymn, cry, exult, exclaim. Nothing else. The dogs sense the hushedness and cock their ears anxiously. A boy rushes past, carrying a brazier of coals for his master's footwarmers and irons. He maneuvers past a floursack-shaped girl souring along with a husbandless scowl. The tumult tumbles into the distance, the faces nearby sliding to far, and sees them all blending into an identity of One.

Then a shaking-metal sound brings them all to a stop. Rhythmic, rustling of iron, over and over. A sound already frightening before its source comes into view, and then—Penitents! Wearing black and red capes with crosses whose backs are opened wide for the whips, they are roped into a chain that walks on feet bloody from spiked balls. Each whip has nine lashes in remembrance of the whips that lashed Christ, each lash tipped with a spiked ball. Bells on their wrists warn away nonbelievers. Some raise crucifixes, others venerate skulls. Their passage is of grotesquery and death as they look out with pain-fierce eyes on the sweet adorations of the street. But the street looks back without remorse–in fact it is disgusted by this enforced fast on the day of the feast. The clankings pass but the street does not revive until two dogs get into a bristling match, growl at each other, and one of them scrunches its shoulders and tucks its tail and scurries half sideways away seeking a refuge, not comprehending why the entire street is throwing rocks at it to drive it out of sight.

The parvis is filling. Josquin Lefief is there with his boys. They have brought a small wagon drawn by two dogs, which has a tiny brick oven built on one end. The glowing coals inside warm their loaves. He moves it where he wants it, then sets up a table with pots of mixed walnut butter and honey his wife has made.

The women of the town arrive in their new clothes. They hold their skirts high in front of them while their daughters trail behind, winding their way awkwardly through the choking streets between the oxcarts and mule posts. Farmers are there selling wine from lumbering barrels bedded on straw and tapped by reed pipettes. Not many customers now, but . . .

And not so far away a tiny plaza is almost filled by one painted wagon and one beribboned horse. Traveling mummers with dark eyes and bright clothes, who walk in Gypsy ways but are not Gypsies, who appeared out of the morning mist to set up their puppets and mime, delighting the children and bringing frowns from adults, only to vanish and not be seen again for decades. Their wagon has a drop leaf on the back that opens up to a tiny stage with tiny curtains of tiny-patterned cloth that swish back and forth as they unfold high words and low deeds in faraway places that somehow seem near, ragged clowns understood only by children, preposterous names and outrageous speeches, pretty ladies and very brave knights. The story spirals to a climax and suddenly the curtain closes just at the fatal blow as a disembodied voice from within says, "He who would know more must be free with his purse." Only on the Feast of the Annunciation could they dare to stay in town for more than three days. Only through the Virgin could life's delicious unlogic be tasted.

The parvis is packed when the first trumpets are heard. The silence is instantaneous. Then again, far out into the echoes, a strident Annunciation blares from alleyways and rooftops. Then a faint unrhythm of drums, tambourines, bells. *Ave* whispers a shivering throat. *Ave!* returns a hundredfold nearby. *AVE!* murmurs the multitude. The sky is hidden in the sun's glare. They swelter in it, feel the heat, think of it not as heat but as sea. A hermit among them issues a prayer from his raspy throat. Trembling in his clothing of woven reeds and coarse raffia, sunken eyed and flat chested, ragged, dirty, infested with ticks, and inexhaustibly holy, even he is awed.

Then banners! Giant panels of color, three men high and four men broad, held aloft by poles and furling thickly in the wind's heave. One red, one blue, one green, one yellow; embroidered fantastically with Man, Lion, Ox, and Eagle: Matthew, Mark, Luke, John. Beneath them are thurifers, white-robed clerks from the local chancery, each waving at the crowd a bronze sphere filled to the top with sweet gums and incense that erupt clouds of smoke and perfume. The smell wafts among the crowd and rises into the air. The banners advance ponderously, each pole grasped by four knights wearing mail and helmets but no swords. They cleave a slow path up to the closed door of the cathedral and fan out one by one along the steps until the mass of the cathedral appears to loom from a façade of brocade. Then come princes, kings, nobles, and ladies, walking outside without hats on for perhaps the only time in their lives. This is the day even they must remove their hats and wait for the door to open.

Then glints of copper shine from a far corner. Josquin climbs on top of his cart and helps up his boys. He puts his arms around them and they twine together into a mass that cannot be swayed. They see the bright flashes again and this time they rise like lances and blare a fanfare not music but Annunciation.

Behind them comes the first of the tribute, the this-world's things given to the next. Each gift arrives with the official that accompanies it: bishop, legate, cardinal, ambassador. Then, "The gift of the Pope! The Rock of Saint Peter!" *Ave* roars the nearest few hundred. *Ave!* returns a thousand. *AVE!* replies the multitude. They imagine the Pope himself smoothing down the coverlets and locking the gold casket. It will be a tabernacle, they know, it couldn't be anything else. A tabernacle of jewels and gold and silver that today will be consecrated with simple water and oil and then opened for the first time. Inside will be a chalice of jewels and gold and silver, containing particles of bread and droplets of wine.

And they know the meaning of these things, of jewels and gold and silver:

Jewels brought from the world's ends, sewn into the ragged cloaks of pilgrims disguised as beggars, who, knowing the ways of the desert and the sea, pray they won't die before seeing again the chapel where their pilgrimage will finally end. And many of them failing. Failing at the col of a pass, too cold to walk any more, the cold so deep it doesn't feel as pain but as sleep. Vanishing without a trace at sea with only imaginings to say what might have been. Feeling the cold blaze which turns instantly to a sear and then the bubbling hiss of a scream that will never reach its throat as the coat is torn off and the boots yanked away and they do not realize what is in the lining of the coat until one of them feels the lump and tries to conceal it but another sees him and they begin fighting and the voice is trying to scream NO! but hears only silence.

Gold taken from springfed pools so high in the mountains that the edge of the water has ice into June but which they have to work anyway, wearing only loincloths and shivering as much from the master's whip as the water's sting. They push hollow reeds into the sediment, cap the ends with their hands, then pull them out and pour the trapped mud into baskets their children carry down to the fire pots, where the glitter is congealed and taken away by men even the slavemasters bow to, away to places they cannot comprehend except to imagine that there too must live men whose eyes have never known hope.

Silver hacked out of the earth's depths by sweating, cursing men. Men working in the reeking smoke of nut-oil lamps, prying loose the exposed seams into baskets their children carry up long rope ladders over ascents too slippery to climb, all of them wordlessly dreading the groan of the earth that makes the air shudder and grow sweeter until the lamps finally gutter and die as the men stand in the blackness holding the broken rope strands and scream.

31

If the gifts did not have agony and redemption, they would not be worthy. And so they come, the jeweled boxes, carved nautilus shells made to look like ships with puffed sails, painted books and silver candleholders, carved ivory crucifixes, maps of the world, chalices, reliquaries.

The parvis fills with the tribute of the world. Chalices for chapels, purple vestments tinctured with the glands of shellfish, carved alabaster, stamped medallions from far princes, lengths of cloth embroidered with bird-quill thread, the finest thread of all. Sapphire, onyx, carbuncle, emerald. Alabaster, porphyry, marble, soapstone. Indigo, orchil, purpura, saffron. They all arrive to wait for the cathedral door to open, but it does not open for them.

Priests in white robes file alongside the gifts, carrying baskets of gold coins which they throw as far as they can into the crowd. The boys there surge forward to scramble on their hands and knees seeking the ones that fall to the ground as the voices in the cloth canyons above shout *Ave!* and the priests reply *Ave Maria Stellis!* The men who have carried their burdens of gold and silver arrive at the steps and turn to face the path She will take and it is hot and they are sweating so they shift their burdens to make themselves more comfortable and begin singing *Ave Maria Stellis.* Sprinklers of holy water walk amid the crowd, flicking their uimpilons out over the faces, and they who feel its touch cry *Ave* while the flingers shout *Ave Maria Stellis!*

Then a column of hooded men arrives amid the roar of a thousand *Ave*s. Members of the Brotherhood of Mercy, devout laymen who serve Her with their identities masked, they are to those who have survived mortal illness the holiest of all. Candle-bearing and caped, they follow no saint's school but walk in saints' ways, working even in the room where the plague still lives, and when they see the buboes on their own skin know there is nothing left for them but to sing hosannas to the Virgin and work until the end.

Ave! they cry.

AVE! thunders the crowd. *Ave!* echoes the cathedral. *AVE!* roars back the multitude. *AVE!* returns the cathedral. They rise into a rhythm of *AVE!* hurled to *AVE!* multiplied by *AVE!* and given to *AVE!* They pick up the pace to greet each echo until the façade of the cathedral trembles with the concussion:

AVE AVE AVE AVE AVE AVE AVE AVE AVE

Still the doors do not open.

This is the volcano the cardinals hear as they arrive in their red robes, carrying Her throne on top of their shoulders. She is heaven jeweled by the earth. Her face is nearly hidden by the crush of their tribute. The air is thick with smoke but Her radiance gleams such a vision that the shouts redouble and then go still higher as the guards press back the surge so Her bearers can pass. Women clasp their house icons and hold them up to Her face and men yell themselves into a frenzy at her childbride's face and the children begin crying as time melts into a stream of pure sound and pure color and the senses shred themselves into nothingness as the roar becomes still louder.

The cardinals reach the bottommost step, then slowly lower Her throne, first in front and then in back, until they are on their knees and prepared to enter Her home. She ascends so slowly that time has no meaning, so radiantly that life is forgotten, so bathed in their joy that the moment vanishes into the immense tremor of Her sea, rising as the sea does, far out on a sea wind. Invisible at first beneath its tiny lappets of swept blue, calling its strengths from out of its depths, then going the wind's way. To swell towards land, becoming first visible far beyond the shoreline's eye as a long, low rise. Lifting and growing, rhythming in on the wind's urge to stumble at first imperceptibly upon the land's rise, its sea hair blown back by the rush of its own strength, pushing forward so far out over itself it breaks up into a rubble of its own roar, it shreds itself up onto the land in streaks of bubbles that hiss to a halt, turn, and begin to glide back, the last fragments of Her dominion a pencil-slim streak of washed sand.

Only then does the door open.

1346

—

Victory

The camp is swarming with looters. The cowards and mercenaries who had deserted when their battle line wavered have now come back to the camp and its tents, discarding their crossbows and pikes on the way. The camp becomes a shambles as they shoulder whatever loot they can find. They hurriedly grasp anything of value, then run toward the bramble-filled ravines where they can hide. They are too frenzied to do anything but yell others away from their hoard as they rifle the packs and kick over the cots.

The camp is on the ridge of a hill. Beyond it in a meadow flee two halves of a headless army. Panic-stricken princes and knights ride near the front, followed by the broken contingents of crossbowmen, archers, harquebusiers, pikemen, executioners, all looking back over their shoulders at the army galloping at them faster than they can run.

Back in the camp the minutes tick by desperately as the deserters grab the last things and flee, always distracted by yet another unopened sack or unexamined tent. But too late! The camp is suddenly overrun by a bellowing mass of horsemen, waving their swords and shouting "Victory! Victory!" as they storm past the tents, flinging them aside with their spears, rushing on toward the big tents, the tents with the flags of the nobles.

The deserters are caught and given their reward. Those still wearing helmets have the visors torn open and their throats cut. Their screams turn to hissing

35

bubbles as they drown in their blood. Others are beheaded by broadswords or are impaled on pikes. The cowards who throw up their hands and plead for mercy are finished mercilessly, as ropes are knotted tightly to their arms and legs and the horses at the other ends are suddenly lashed and run in startled panic until the ropes run out and the cowards are torn to pieces amid the laughter of the victors.

The sack begins. Boxes of loot are axed open and saddlebags are slit. Gold spills, rich cloth bursts out, jewels fall into the blood, presided over by pleading camp guards praying on their knees who within a few minutes are dead, their heads axed off and spitted on pikes raised high to witness the sack.

Rough yells, coins, running feet. Tents burst into flames, wine barrels tip over, and men drink straight from them, streaming red rivers over their beards. Dying horses lie on their sides flailing the dust, uncomprehending, dizzy with terror and death. A hanged man is cut down amid roars of laughter, some offender of discipline delivered by a victory that for him has come too late. His body is replaced by a struggling, white-eyed fat man, the camp's panderer, who once too often lorded over them his access to the camp women. Now his hands are powerless, tied behind his back, and he babbles that if he can go free he'll tell them where he's hidden his treasure.

But they know they'll find it anyway, so his eyes bulge as he feels the rope's iron clench and he sees the men below popping off his pant buttons with sword tips. His pants fall off and his legs kick wildly for the ground just out of reach, his tongue moving soundlessly as they laugh and tell him his neck is going to learn how big his belly is and he feels the terrible blackness coming on, wishing it would hurry so this would be over.

In the lower camp, the panderer's camp, the camp of cushions on make-shift cots, the victory is greeted with the false screams of those who alone will prosper from the victors: the prostitutes. They know the first men will take them, but the later ones will pay.

To a different camp, in a secluded vee where a little creek flows, victory comes differently. The wives of the nobles are there, deserted by their retainers, wearing their wealth in necklaces and rings. Their girls, the maids and cleaning women, are raped and then thrown into a ditch. The ladies themselves, assembled in their finery, dignified and possessed, also will be raped, but it will be by their own class, it will be called service, it will be done with respect, and it will not be mentioned when negotiating their ransom.

The creek they stand alongside flows down into a stream, and that stream runs red. Fleeing men still in their armor are speared by pikemen on horses. Others slip on the wet stones and fall in, but are trapped under its surface by the weight of their armor, drowning in knee-deep water their fingers can escape but their lips cannot. Nearby tree limbs are bowed with strangling men, their tongues blue and eyes white in the gouge of hanging's fingers. The last few of the vanquished, who had tried to hide in trees, are shot down by crossbowmen and ended with swords. In the nearby hamlet of Crecy, peasant huts burn, filling the air with the greasy smoke of hay and wood and animals trapped inside.

When the day ends, the camp has finished burning and the blood has crusted in pools and the tents have been trampled into the blood. Only the wine remains, and the victorious army drinks it in full. Mouthful after mouthful, they drunken themselves as quickly as they can, count and hoard their coins, then fling them down in the dice pits. Fires heaped high with wreckage crackle and smoke as the men go off, heads reeling, to slip in the slime, vomit, and yell, "Crecy! Crecy! Victory! Victory!"

1349

The Abbey's Used Waters

Boniface Lefief, nicknamed The Delver, makes his daily survey of the abbey's waters. A man of few words but great oaths, he accepted reluctantly the post of Master of the Stream to which the abbot had appointed him. He was a proud man, a man who could count the names of his ancestors on both hands and one foot. But the abbot knew the will of God, and the abbot said God's will was that Boniface should become the finest delver the abbey had ever known. Now as he makes his daily inspection of the waters, Boniface reflects on how the abbey's form had been chosen to channel the stream's flow into the most uses possible.

The river arrives through a conduit under the abbey's north wall. When the water emerges, it is in the shadow of the abbey church. There a large sluice diverts part of it, which slides along a millrace to jet against the paddles of a huge wheel. Cone-shaped wooden gears change the millrace's horizontal flow into the vertical spin of a shaft, at the bottom of which is a stone larger around than the span of a man's arms. It turns against a fixed bottom stone, and in its slot wheat and barley grains are cracked, crushed, and spun into flour.

The millrace continues only a pace before it strikes another paddle wheel. This one's shaft has large, many-lobed cams on its end, which strike against a wooden box with a perforated leather bottom. As flour from the mill flows into the box, the paddle wheel turns the shaft, which shakes the box, which sifts the flour through the perforations, which leaves the husks and bran behind.

The sluice rejoins the river's main flow just above the formal gardens of the friars' dorter, or dormitory. There long poles on swivels swing out over the flow, drop buckets into the water with a splash, then lift them out again brimming with water for the garden's fresh flowers and herbs.

A few steps further on, another branch is sluiced off. It ristles its way along a stone conduit that runs first in the open, then under stone walkways, slipping invisibly under walls and outbuildings, emerging in the vast stone-columned arcade of the cloister that is the heart of the abbey. There, under the open sky, the friars work, recite their prayers, stroll, do small tasks such as mending their frocks and sandals. The conduit passes the stalls of the scriptorium, where the older friars work in quiet retirement making documents and books. Then it empties into an octagonal pool in the center of the cloister. Here the friars fill their ewers and basins in the morning, then turn back to their cells to bathe.

Boniface nods silently to the friars, then bends to pluck a few errant blades of grass trying to gain a foothold between the thick hexagonal tiles of the walkway. He curses the tufts angrily before stuffing them into a leather pouch hanging from the thongwork of his belt. His words startle the friars within earshot. Thinking he is oathing them, they whisper to each other and bolt the doors to their cells.

The remaining water spills through small spouts on each face of the cloister pool into a channel running around the bottom. This flows into another conduit that runs diagonally across the cloister, beneath its southern walkway and the clerks' offices beyond, emerging on the periphery only to tumble into another sluice, this one serving the infirmary.

Here the largest portion of the sluice branches off immediately toward the kitchens beyond, but a smaller branch flows down a short incline into a square stone pool, where a friar occasionally fetches water from it with a bucket. The bucket sinks and is hoisted out dripping, to be taken away for bathing and to steep the active ingredients in herbs, roots, and tree barks they use as medicines.

Then, its purity no longer important, the pool's water flows into a spout and thence to a second basin. This one, scummy with tallow film, is the infirmary's washtub. Nearby, attached to a trellis ascending a wall, hempen twines sag under the weight of dripping cassocks, frocks, and sheets. The frocks are hung upside down so that the tatters that will result from their having been bunched and tied tightly by the twines will not be noticeable amid the frays of coarse cloth constantly being dragged on the ground. Lighter garments are held up with clothespins made of split cane. Boniface attends to a dozen or so which have fallen on the ground. He reattaches them to the twisted hemp, cursing what manner of friar it is who thinks a delver should tend to clothespins as if a washerwoman.

The laughter and light chatter from inside the infirmary mingle with the soft sounds of water eddying in the pool. Inside, several friars are having their quarterly bleeding, to purge the humours that bring lust. It is a happy time for them, for they have been relieved of their duties for a week and get all the meat and wine they want. It is a time for shedding burdens, when true thoughts may be expressed (for are they not ill?), and they listen to one another's tales all the way through.

The branch that leads south into the kitchen undergoes a less leisurely fate. Its water tumbles from a spout that penetrates the kitchen wall near the door, splashing noisily into a stone trough that hugs the entire length of one wall, more than a dozen paces long. On the opposite side is an equally long fireplace.

The trough is divided into three basins, each lower than the previous. The first is the smallest, and contains water for cooking and drinking. The next is for rinsing. Above it are pegs, hooks, and a series of crude iron racks. On these, respectively, towels dry, sooty clothes are hung, and the kitchen's spits, pots, forks, knives, whisks, ladles, trivets, and basins are stacked up to dry. Alongside, a rack holds long, flat blades of iron used to spit meat and game birds for roasting next to the fire. Boniface scoops up a wisp of fat congealed along the rim of the rinsing trough, wipes it onto his leggings, and oaths about so careless a kitchen crew that they have come to think others should complete their work.

Finally the water flows over a U-shaped efflux into the third and largest basin, the basin used for washing. Above it is a row of wooden boxes, or *fourmes*, which word in time came to describe the shallow wooden buckets used to curdle cheese, thence to the word for the making of cheese, *fourmage*, and finally the word for cheese itself, *fromage*.

One of the wooden fourmes is filled with the abbey's homemade soap—a mixture of rendered fat, oil, and ashes that is scooped out by the handful to clean the grease film off fire-blackened pots. Another has sand in it, for scouring off dried food and the crust of the abbey kitchen's ever-present burnt cheese. The last is stacked with lens-shaped white ovals of cuttlefish spines, which were washed up on distant seashores and collected by itinerant pedlars who sell them as a soft abrasive for copper.

Boniface's inspection of the water's grease-filmed exit is unheard amid the din of cauldron clangs, roaring fires, clattering spoons, shouted instructions, and the splattery sound of fat bursting from roasts into the flames.

Beyond these buildings, the stream begins to gather back the murky trickles from its branches. But its work is still not yet done. Beyond the square of the main part of the abbey is the small cluster of the abbot's quarters. His buildings are also cloistered in a square, just as Roman buildings once did to keep them warm in winter and shaded in summer.

The largest building is the atrium, the abbot's offices, where the abbey's records, documents, and treasury are kept. A lesser building attached to it is the locutorium, where guests are received. Next to it is the scriptorium, where the friars gather during cold winter evenings to play games, talk, or write. Here the river's water is brought in thimbles, to pour into inkwells. The ink is thinned so that if it is applied for a second time the thicker stroke will reveal the presence of a correction or attempted forgery.

Abutting the abbey's main gate in the west wall (so visitors would enter in the same direction they would face if departing for Jerusalem), a small rivulet of the stream spills into a basin alongside the abbot's personal quarters. Attached to his residence are the abbey's stables, wine cellar (locked with two locks), and the sacramenoria, wherein are kept the chalices of gold, jeweled vestments, silver monstrances, and altar silks. The river does not flow here, it is carried in carafes to thin the consecrated wine.

Still the water's utility is not done. Beyond the abbot's quarters, butted against the abbey's south wall, are work sheds. On its way there, the river first passes through the abbey's gardens. Small wooden gates only slightly larger than a hand

divert the flow into channels that rim the edges of more than a dozen rectangular plots, each bordered with boxwood to keep out nighttime's prowling animals.
Graveled walkways lead between them, this plot for the infirmary's medicinal
plants, that one for kitchen herbs, another for garlic, still others for the fruits,
vegetables, and nuts that cannot be demanded from the peasant landholders outside the walls. Along the abbey's entire east wall is a row of walnut trees which
break the harsh winds of November and March. Beneath them is a sprawling,
unmanaged patch of vines, whose grapes are not for wine but for the table—and
for verjuice while still green, an astringent better than vinegar to whiten fish or
fowl. In the middle of the garden is a gazebo for hot days, constructed of timbers and climbing glycines lashed together with leather thongwork. A trickle of
the river passes here in a slim channel, to be dipped out to quench a thirst or
smooth rough workaday wine.

Then the river flows toward the sheds. Here at last is Boniface at home.
He relaxes for the first time since his daily inspection began. The men here are
men such as himself, fiefmen whose poverty came by birth rather than vow. Now
suddenly he laughs and is loquacious as he gathers them and assigns each a tool
as they prepare to go outside the walls.

Their party passes several channels, ruder that any of those before, which
angle off to pools. One is deep and in it the friars bathe during the summer.
Another flows into a paddle wheel, again turning an axle. This axle also ends
in irregular wooden ovals. These turn beneath several wooden mallets. As the
oval ends rise, so do the mallets, and as they drop, they thump against a stump-
end that rests in a trough filled with wads of cloth remaining after the friars' cassocks have worn through. A friar sits at the edge, poking a large carved wooden
spoon carefully among the rising and falling mallets, arranging the cloth continu-
ally until it has been pounded into its elemental fibers.

These fibers are dumped into a vat filled with water, and the whole is stirred
until it is soupy and uniform. Another friar dips into this soup a flat wooden rec-
tangle which has a metal screen across its open center. The screen is made of
hundreds of wires that catch up the cloth threads in the soup and, when shaken,
form them into an even, flat mass. He trims away the irregularities on the form's

edges, lifts it out, turns it quickly upside down so the matted fiber sheet falls onto the flat surface of a *pressoir*, which is then screwed down until moisture stops running out its edges. In a few moments he unscrews the *pressoir* and peels away from its bottom surface a thin, damp, new sheet of paper and droops it over a rack to dry.

Another channel flows to the tannery. Its water splashes into a large trough where new hides soak for several weeks so their hair can be loosened and stripped off. Part of the water is diverted to fill several carved stone basins, where it slowly dissolves the plant barks and flower petals that will later dye the leather. In other vats, broader and less deep, the scraped hides are soaked for a week in a brine of coarse salt, oak bark, and horse urine. The newly tanned leather is then rinsed in a rapidly flowing part of the stream, dyed, and rinsed again. A final trough rinses away the last of putridness and color, and the new leather is stretched to dry in the shade. Then it is rolled up in bundles tied with thongs to be taken to the sandal-making shed.

There are other channels. They take the stream's water to the forge, the carpenter's, the barrelmaker's, the hot baths used in winter, the troughs of the stable, and the waist-high carved stone tubs where friars come to wash their frocks if it isn't their allotted laundry day.

The river leaves the abbey in a conduit under the south wall. Not quite yet joined of all its parts, it is bridged by one last building. This is made of light-colored stone and has stained glass windows along its eaves. There, having been used by everyone to perform all the deeds that water can perform—washing, watering, diluting, rotating, powering, scouring, cooling, bathing, cleaning, quenching, pleasing ears as it passes, giving itself freely—and having bubbled up into fountains, spilled over small dams, flowed through gates, swirled around vats, splashed up onto faces, it departs the abbey with a gurgle and a swish, taking with it the amassed residues of all the abbey's activities as it passes beneath the last building of all, the modest enclosure of the necessarium.

And here gather the rats which have come upstream, attracted by the rich, complex odors of the water leaving the abbey. They fight and squeal here, expel and accept newcomers, procreate, and are driven off briefly by Boniface's workmen, who have come to repair the stones of the abbey wall's foundations. But, being rats, they are as proprietary as the abbey itself, and they fight equally harshly when threatened. One, cornered by Boniface jabbing at it with a spade, has no choice but to flee between his legs. As the rat passes it gnashes out fiercely with its teeth, gouging through Boniface's leggings and into his flesh. Boniface winces, oathes, kills the rat with his spade, then resumes his work.

Within a day, after having mingled with a third or more of the abbey's friars or retinue, he becomes feverish and notices his underarms are painful and hot. He is soon in agony and screams again and again for water, and within two days is dead. Being a workman and not a friar, he is buried with no pomp. The friars of the infirmary who come to deliver his last rites speak momentarily of the odd-colored swellings under his arms and the excruciating way he passed, attribute it to his choleric temper with its symptomatic signs of black-spirited mutterings and oaths, then go back to the century-old tranquillity the stream has brought into their walls.

1440

The Rosary

But for thirty-odd lines in St. Luke, no one would have known of the Virgin's existence. She was reported in Nazareth, at the marriage at Cana, at the foot of the Cross, in a handful of other places, and that was all. No one could even say when or where she died.

Now, fourteen hundred years later, she is the uniting radiance of the Church, surpassing her son, God, and all the martyrs and saints. More than half the churches in Christendom are dedicated to her. Knights and soldiers praise her name as they cut each other to bits. The theologians of Paris debate whether she possessed perfectly the seven Liberal Arts, which include science and economics. Towns all over Christendom vie for which prays to her in the most worshipful way.

The friar Adam de la Roch had heard that the folk of a certain French town over the years had devised a ritual they called the rosary, a simple cycle of prayers to the Virgin chanted by churchgoers in unison. Adam was ambitious, and like many friars of his time, knew well the example of Francis of Assisi, who created a following so large it begat him sainthood.

Now Adam stands on a low bluff overlooking this town, seeing its history spread away like a map. It had grown out of an ancient ford where shallow water ran swiftly over small stones, making it easy for animals to cross. At one tip of the town a smaller stream braids itself in. The first hamlet grew on this spit of land, soon growing prosperous enough to build a tollkeeper's house, a wooden gate, stone walls, a public bread oven, a granary.

Where the two waters joined there was a bastide, a fortified church with arrow-slit windows and a flat-topped tower full of crenellations. In the rough centuries after the Church proclaimed the Peace of God, priests nonetheless built thick walls. What it was like under attack hardly can be imagined. The entire village would be trembling within, arrows hissing through the windows, great fires in the corners, men dying with their wives shrieking beside them, everyone praying the doors would hold.

Now it is little used. There are bird nests in the eaves and part of its thick outer wall is shattered, remnant of some long-forgotten breach. In front of it is the first market square, scarcely larger than two or three houses, where some of the nearby farmers still come with their cabbages and eggs. Around the square, bent-timbered old houses hold each other up like a parade of drunk angles, half-thatch, half-air.

The old bourg huddled under the bastide church. No one can now say how long it took for the town to grow. But at some point there came an empty time, perhaps of war or plague or a grasping line of local lords, and the place where its growth stopped is more evident than the when. Two houses have collapsed. Another is a stone shell containing the remnants of charred beams. Overgrown orchards nearby, fruitless and bare-limbed, crumbled fences, a well without a bucket, the empty church records of people who died without seeing their grandchildren.

Beyond these old-town remnants now turned into garden plots and old dogs behind fences, there is the green of a broad commons where the sheep and cattle are still herded at night. At its edge is a small enclosure behind walls. A new granary and hayrick there speak of the vigor of the new bourg. A bridge, a stable, a carved stone wellhead with four spouts, the tollkeeper's new quarters with room enough for ten men. These are bright times, with the officials importing stonecutters to build a bridge over the ford, a powerful lord extending his castle, a traveling smith setting his son up with a permanent forge, and villagers surging in and out of the market. Stone houses now appear alongside those of wood: houses whose shutters are now flung open, flying housemaids' flags of the linen being aired.

The old town's church was a church of the sword. The new town's church is a church of the Virgin. It has slim arches and a steeple like hands pointed in prayer, carved wooden chancel screens surrounding the altar to keep the flock at a distance from the priest. Its flamboyance marks the dawn of a new time: the mother in a manger becomes the Queen of Paradise.

Near the new church, a silent market cross gazes down on a noisy square. This market is ten times larger that the old bourg's, and even has its own timbered roof. It has booths for moneychangers and shoemenders, herbsellers and soapmakers, barbers, linen shops, lockmakers, lace. Banners hang out from the shopfronts, the buildings that soar next highest to the church. Their windows tell of the social order within: the lace-curtained floor of Monsieur and Madame, above them the linen curtains of the children, then the oiled-paper windows of grandmere and the aunts, and finally the tiny circle of the maids' quarters, cramped under the thatch eaves, dank and cold during winter, and reeking of smoke from a leak in the chimney. Behind, at the bottom of a crooked stairs used by the help, water laps from a wellhead into a stone trough for the laundry. Threadbare smocks hang there from pegs, smelling of flowery scent. Madame buys soap now from the shops, for the family no longer keeps cattle, and the scented olive-oil soaps from Castile are finer by far.

Roads spread away from the square, passing first the houses of the cloth-sellers and butchers, angling past the simpler shops of candlemakers and horse-meat sellers. There the wooden walkway ends. Beyond lie the shops of the crafts-men, the glowing forge of the smith, the huts of the poor and the shoemenders and seamstresses, the old women whose men have gone, the last of the bakers, on out to the irregular shanties of the half-townsmen/half-peasants who dwell on a town's edges—cartdrovers, haysellers, stablehands, wallmenders, ditchdig-gers, eggsellers, butchers, poachers.

Across the river is a cultivated area of rolling hillocks, checkered with the tiny plots of townsmen's gardens, each walled off from the other with wattle fences of woven reeds. Each has a gateway with a lock and a bower under a tree. The path to these fields follows the river's bank, touching down to water's edge at fishing wiers and anglers' stumps, then retreating inland around inlets and ponds.

A faint squall catches Adam's ear and he seeks out its direction. Half-hidden in the mist-thin distance, in the middle of a field on the other side of town, he sees round tents and clusters of people. There wafts another tendril of sound, and this time it's a tune. A *loure* is there, a countryman's bagpipe, and he lets it guide him as he meditates on the rosary as he enters the soundscape between the town's cobbles and roofs.

These are November sounds, the sounds of a town preparing for winter. The path down from the bluff begins with a light concerto of finches, swelling to a cow carillion against a sheep meadow of munches. Wash water and the contents of chamber pots hit the road with a thick *swopp*. Whispery sounds scurry from an old woman on her way to the well, fastpatter sandalscuffs vanishing into the giant dull thuds of an oxcart plod. Masons' chisels clink away at bricks to break them in the right place, a carpenter's adze gouges as he shapes a new yoke for an ox, cleaning women whistle in their breath as they brace for the weight of their buckets. Sausage sellers rearrange their bins, to the whiney impatience of mongrels.

The town may seem chaotic to the eye, but the ear remakes it into a midafternoon chord: hay rustlings, donkey beatings, coin slaps on barrel tops, haggles over eggs, horse wheezes, boy yells, bellow hissings, bare feet padding along on some mission of urgency, linen ruffles as bedding is taken in from windows, dustcloth exclamations. Milkmaids urge along their slow charges with tapping sticks and muttered *hyoop*s. A ragpicker pulls along his broken-wheeled cart, clacking over the stones as he rings his bell and sings his song. A furiously clattering official's wagon careens to a halt, and a footman's steps gurgle in the mud as he rushes to the door. Two cackles and a cluck signal precedence between the hens as they nibble at a bundle of greens tied to a string in the middle of a doorway, exactly peck-high.

The square is emptying, beckoned by the snake charm of the loure. Adam observes the tiny moments of near silence that break the town's euphony, silences resting lightly on day's end. Flies hover over broken fruit. A woman cracks mustard seeds with the back of a spoon. Five bold bongs from the new town clock are followed by a quiet protest of four from the neglected steeple down in the old bourg. A man with a wooden leg hesitates to cross a street and patiently waits until a deliveryman's donkey clips on by, then finally dares, clinging in half-panic to his rustling basket of breads.

The sounds of the market tell as well of faces and shapes. A heavy-bearded sign painter speaks over his sketches in a voice that draws the eye to its power. He talks of composition, harmony, color, balance . . . prices. A slurry of flaxen sounds blurs from a basket weaver on her way home. The rustle of leaves in a gutter marks a cat intent on closing in on a bird. A chomp goes by, holding in its hand an apple. Hair swept back and clinched by a pin, a merchant's daughter dressed in black brushes past the others, swishing her cape in a haughty flow of wrist. Two chatterers pass their way home, ripe and full of giggling, swathed in bodices a father's frown too tight. A clicking swash announces a young lord, adjusting his sword and saluting his broad hat as he acknowledges the tipped hats of passersby. The smoking volcano of a newlywed's argument seethes past on a low heat, words spitting from the tight fissures of their lips. Then a sexy young butcher's apprentice comes wine-sliding along, laughing uproariously as he winks at a flax heap of concubine hair.

Then Adam hears the hunched scrape of a cripple. Bent from a bad birth, she propels her tangled body using a wooden-handled shoe formed to fit her hand, pulling the rest of her along on a sled strapped to what remains of her legs, so frail she could be blown away by pieces of the wind and yet so iron she will be bent forever. She drags behind her a sack of plucked flowers, and sings to the mud:

> I don't know where to begin
> To tell the troubles I've been.
> But I've grass for your sleep,
> It's not pity I seek.
> Give Marie Lefief a sou,
> And she'll be gone.

51

A pillow stuffer, surviving on what grass she can sell to travelers who will fold their neckerchief into a square, fill it with this grass and fold it again into a pillow. Adam beckons to her, gives her a coin. She beams and clasps her hands toward heaven. Her voice is a sparrow, of God telling the world that as He makes all He accepts all.

Gramercy, kind Sire. 'Tis a long night ahead and it is enough for sleep to have grass for your head. My belly is filled past bearing with hunger. There's not many that sleep on grass any more. It's such a good sleep! And I've got a good bunch of roots, too. You can bake them with wet leaves in the stones of your fire. They be a small meal, but that is the fare of our sins! Eve snatched Paradise from the hands of her children and ate the apple that took the world. But the Virgin! The Virgin will love us! She is so beautiful, so very beautiful. It is everything I live for that someday I will see her. Haven't I told you before? She's more beautiful than anything we know, even the flowers! The loveliest bride in all heaven! God himself chose to live in her womb! In Jerusalem they said, "She has conceived without a husband, you know what maketh her that." And she said, "Eve's sin is forgiven, God has come to us through a woman!" We souls, we will be waiting outside the gate, still in our chains, thinking only of ourselves and what she may say to us. And then unto us she will come! God himself will shine behind her, the Almighty and his Son! And *Her*! Sitting on a gold cloth and wearing a gold crown. Looking on us and blessing us! She will give us white robes and she will release us and thank us and we will sing and we will *rise!*

The rest of the town passes in a flurry of banners. Then Adam passes the granary onto the grass of the field. The bagpiper is still squalling his brocaded tattoo. His cheeks puff into a wooden tube and under his arm he holds a pigskin that's been sewn tight enough to hold a lungful of air. Two pipes come out to loop over his shoulder, with tassels on the end and a foxtail between. These pipes moan the tonic tones around which his fingers string the tune. What he lacks in rhythm he makes up for in imaginings, fingers chasing out notes as thick as mosquitoes in midsummer.

A chain dance forms, a serpentine mingling of colors and necklaces and hands. Young girls are the first to begin dancing, practicing with each other to get the steps right, then trying to unloosen the knots of boys around the crowd's edges, the bowlines of faces that can be untied with the eyes.

A moon-faced flutist joins the piper with a nod. With a bob of his head he catches the pace, then wails high a soprano world racing faster than time into the night. Beneath him a tambourine begins, and that brings in the clomp of wooden shoes and slaps on bent knees. The piper hurls out the first few notes of a catch, and the flutist goes still faster to garnish them with grace notes and trills. Then the embroidery thins and their notes glide out onto a song. It's an old tune the entire town knows. It is so smooth it makes them all wish they were a snake—and so they are: arms link and unfurl in the sly sex of the S-dance. The girls' seriousness softens from doing it right to doing it for fun, dancing them-selves into a riot of melting colors.

A reedy oboe joins the platform as the town's pillars gather their wives to go home to the uncertain solace of their portraits and mirrors. The mood of the dance changes from curtseys to swung arms. Spangle sounds come from wrist-bells and aprons fly. A kiss slides by halfway through a turn, and a surprised face vanishes away into the two-step beyond. Bonnets fall and are snatched up in midbeat, hair shakes loose in the tremble of the tune. A proud potbelly launches into a reel, turning a quick four-step into a two-step glide carried with such aplomb it is almost like grace. Another kiss is grabbed, this time held for a handful of beats. A baby's chin is tickled as it sucks on its teething toy, a sack of mint tied in a cloth. A ball-shaped wad of wool stuffed with damp grass escapes from a circle of playing boys and rolls lumpily into the dance. A dozen feet field it and it goes spurting back out. Two or three women wear a curious necklace made of beans strung in five groups of ten with a white bean between, looping into a circle that has a cross at one end. A group of old men have dressed in outlandish costumes—boots erupting grasses and pants stuffed gigantically with leaves, held up by waistbands twined out of flowers. They kiss a toothless old woman and with exaggerated bows lead her to the edge of the dance, holding her arms up in an imitation sarabande. She remembers most of

NOT BY BREAD ALONE

the old steps, dancing at half the pace of the younger folk but with the same eyes.

Now the dance breaks loose from the chain. They link elbows two by two and weave a complicated knot that ends in a circle. A bow to the right, curtsey to the left, then left foot out, into the pivot and then the turn, ending face-out and wrinkling their noses in mock despair. But the bagpiper knows it's only for eight beats and shakes out a bagful of tunes. The dancers spin and rush to link up arms for the turn. Wristbells flow into cuffs, beltpurses and wineskins swash in a skirt sea. They swoop a hand-exchange over their heads and are back to the original pairs when a last sprinkle of grace notes gives way to a wheeze. The dancers bow and smile in the sudden vast silence of the song's end. A wad of grass goes unfurling through the air, falling over a couple of young lovers to tease them for dancing too tightly.

Adam notices that to these commonplace people commonplace things seem the most important. A loose headdress is about to fall from its pin so three women rush to refit it. Mothers who gossip always smooth their aprons as they do. Wine-keg men who primp their hair are the first to be sick from having too much. Merchants always furrow their brows when they speak of the future. Women who've had many children wear unshapely fashions made of thick cloth. Young men who've never known a woman sew their codpieces with different colored threads. A young woman's embroidery is always the most elaborate over her sex.

Enough! Adam knows what is to be done if these people are to be saved! He leaves the dance in the light of the setting sun, finds a bower by a stream, seats himself on the grass pillow the cripple Marie made for him, and writes:

The Rosary shall be called the Divine Psaltery. It must be prayed so that it consists of a cycle of 150 Ave Marias and fifteen Paternosters. Its divine numerology consists of the Eleven Celestial Spheres plus the Four Elements multiplied by the Ten Categories. This gives us its 150 Natural Habits. Multiplying the Ten Commandments by the Fifteen Virtues gives us its 150 Moral Habits.

Each of the Natural Habits is a queen whose nuptial bed is one of the divisions in the Paternoster ("Our Father / Who Art In Heaven / Hallowed Be Thy Name," and so on). Each word in the Ave Maria signifies a Perfection of the Virgin. Each Perfection is symbolized by the precious stone which may be employed to drive away the animal symbolizing the sin governed by that Perfection. Each Perfection represents one branch of the Tree that carries the Blessed Ones, together with the Steps on which Christ ascended on his way to meet Pilate.

Thus, take the first word: *Ave. Ave* is the first word in Ave Maria. It means "Hail." Hence it is the symbol of the Virgin's innocence, the girl who is unlike any other girl, on whom an angel came calling using that word. The stone of *Ave* is the diamond, for nothing can be purer, and its beast is the lion, for nothing can be more courageous. The lion represents the sin of Pride.

The next word, *Maria*, symbolizes Mary's wisdom, the fact that her knowledge of things came directly from God. *Maria*'s stone is the ruby, symbolizing the pomegranate-hued tears she shed for the droplets of her Son's blood; its beast is the black dog, symbolizing the sin of envy.

The third word is . . .

Hours later, the summation of his life now written, Adam relaxes and dreams of what he will be. He will invent a new order of friars. He will name it the Universal Brotherhood of the Divine Psaltery. He will preach in every hamlet! He will convert Christendom to the rosary! He will be blessed! He will be beatified! He will be a saint!

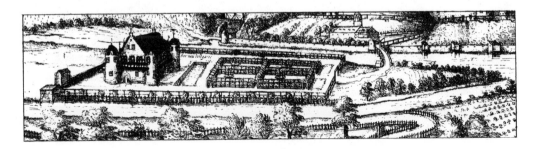

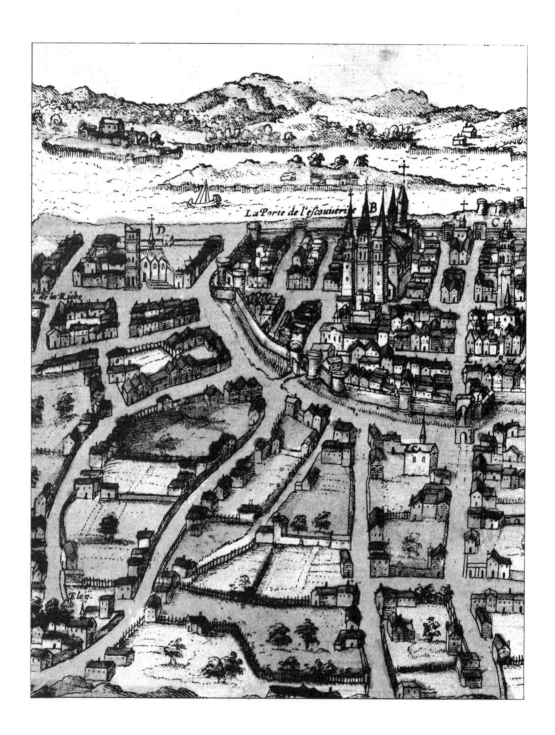

1483

Baptism

On the way to the baptism, they did not yet know what to name him. He was their thirteenth, the seventh of the males. The mother considered these to be auspicious numbers and prayed he would be the last. Still, she could not think of a name.

The coughing clouds of a ragged dawn find them walking the familiar league to the church, clothes next to castoffs kept alive with rough threads. They pass Valcheve, the trodden earth of the community winnowing ground now riven with springtime shoots from wheat that fell into its cracks last fall. A few moments beyond they pass through Chaillou, where once a procession of penitents had passed, so time out of mind ago that a village grandmother's mother heard of it from her grandmother's mother when she was a child, yet she recollects the penitents, their crosses, their whips, as if they were here today. Then to the low grove of Bacherie, where each spring flocks of squalling speckled blackbirds gather, following devils in search of lost souls. A few paces further on are the woodcutter's trestles of Clopard, surrounded by chips and the smell of bark. Then to Pennaxie, where once long ago a shepherd named Pennax listened to the knotted whistle of raptor wings as two overhead hawks culled and divided their prey, the sound of which he turned into a panpipe tune still played at village dances.

They halt momentarily at the distant sound of a bell calling for the prayers of prime at dawn. They kneel. To make up time—for they must be at the church when the jays first begin to call—they walk still faster, even though the baby's head swings too heavily against its swaddle.

Past Rochinerie, the Rockery, where on the day of creation, as the angels were carrying the world's entire supply of stones in a sack, the sack leaked, raining down the curious round rocks all over the floor of this valley, which masons now come to gather to fill the empty space between house walls. Then they are at Combes, where once there lived a man who believed the key to fortune was not to spend a sou; in one of the rarest events of the time, his wife left him. Past Turpiniere, a once renowned abbey now dwindling away its patrimony in a version of saintliness not what it used to be. Across Guillotiere, the pasture where from Christmas to May the weak cattle are brought to die. To Armeaux, where the Gypsy carts with their jingling horse bells always come to ford the stream; and Malvaudieres, where the early spring grapevines twist always to the left.

The pious old one straightens her scarf, a withered hand murmuring its creases. The others are flowers trudging out their time, bearing the child in their only piece of good cloth. They pass other place names on the road to the church, each only a few paces to a hundred paces in length, each with its own heritage of legend or lore, about which the further they walk from their hamlet, the less they know. Already many legends have become faint and they know the place names only for their character—Vertiere (where moss clings to stones, making them bright green), Tauperie (where moles rustle between the fallen chestnut leaves and the earth), Bouchardiere (a meadow of lone pines and dry grasses), Filetieres (where a stream hisses its protest in yielding around a patch of stones), Bertiniere and Boutiniere (both named after their flowers), Perrons, Origeaux, Aurons (where an herb named ybright is gathered to use for anointing and making faces fair), Bourgauderie, Lac Mousseau (a swampy grove of birches and ferns), Pierres (where the stonecutters work), Forge (where the ironmonger sets up his bellows when he is in between fairs), Les Mellieres (the best two fields within a two-league walk—foul fall him who fouls the flowers there!), Huberdelliere, Fromagerie (where the goat-cheese makers live), Coupilliere, Dangerie (the defile above a canyon stream where once a child fell to its death), Guijardiere, Granes,

Barigonniere, Roulliere, Couloire, Planderies, Bourdes, Hardonniere, and finally Carroi, the crossroads, where they take the left road—now a rutway of spring mire—to the church.

The road smells of the season and of mules and the muds of a whole year. They wish the sun didn't need to sleep such long nights, yet when its warmth comes at last, no one of them says a thing.

Having now passed Carroi, they also pass the last place names of which they know the stories. The way from here to the town and its church is a blur of footsteps and lusterless titles—Fontenils, Maconniere, Blandiniere, Vacherie, Bertholonniere, Durandrie, Belasserie, Brulots, Fougeres, Tauche, Bouguerie, Salverte, Riviere, Gimondrie, Gropheteau, Mortiere, Rabottelliere, Saut-en-loup, Beaucaire, Boussardiere, Vallette, Pailletterie, Guignetiere, Ebats, Gaubertiere, Jagonniere, Croix Blanche, Chambord, Champ-verte, Ermitage, Teilles, Pinarderie, Blotiere, Chaponniere, Chenaye, Planches, Trois Cheminees, Reignere, Batisse, Bellonniere, Renardieres, Hustaudries, Raguiniere, Bejauderie, Bergerair, Cosnelle, Sablons, Grieves, Mottes, Bouguerie, Duports, Landes, Boisviniere, Arpiniere, Marais, Friches, Episettes.

Then they pause to shift the child from the mother to one of the other women, and remark the place name, Daviderie, as one they will remember for this event the next time they pass. Then past Murier, past Boutiniere, past Coldreau, Aurons, Benetrie, Vaugaudry, Villeneuve (closer to the town now, they sigh in relief), Croix, Sauvegrain, Bonivet—now the names are becoming village names as they first glimpse in the distance the spire of the church—Avoine, Fourneau (the village bake oven), Fontenay, Lavoir, Sanglier, Chateau.

They come first to the thatched huts, then to the timbers and brick, and they are humbled by the height and the whirl, the noise and the eyes. They pass through town like a vapor, the little one too, leaving behind them but a few lines in a book inked by a priest's pen.

He meets them in the east portal where the morning light is the warmest. As they come up the steps he smiles and starts talking. Then he leads them to the altar, where there is a book and some salt. When the child cries from

59

the sudden bitterness on its tongue, he laughs and asks how it is that such a little creature can make such a big sound.

"If salt were to lose its saltiness, young one, with what would you season?"

Then he asks the name, and the name is Lefief.

"No, no!" he says, "the name of the child!"

The name is David.

"David?! 'David' means 'Courage'," the priest says to the mother, "Did you know that?"

Then he sings the name high: "David . . . Daviiid . . . Daviiiiiid . . . ," curling the name through a plainsong's old chant.

Then a whisper: "David! You're going to be *alive* now! 'Blessed are they who need the Kingdom of God,' and little one, do you realize you could get there before *me*?!"

He smiles at them and they cautiously smile in return. A plain priest wrapped in plain cloth, bathed in plain light. His talk burbles through their silence, a talk of childhood things, of delight, curiosity, daring, boyhood.

" 'David' means 'Courage' but it means other things, too. When the Disciples came to Jesus and asked who was the greatest and the highest in Heaven, he called a child before them. 'I tell you this,' he said, 'unless you are like children you will never enter the kingdom of heaven.' Then he gathered the children before him and he blessed them."

Then a long, ringing, exultant "Daviiiid!," filling the chapel with the name of this new life. He sprinkles water over the child's face, fingerflicking the last few droplets over the parents and others. They anxiously giggle with their hands over their mouths, then nudge each other when the child makes a small sound.

"He is the one being born unto God, but the water of life was meant for us all. David . . . Oh David . . . Oh Daviiid . . . Oh DaVie . . . Eau de Vie. This child of life is the water of life. Such a thirst can be quenched only from an eternal spring's flow."

Afterward, the words, the ceremony, the markings on paper, the held hands. He opens the huge doors for them, to the brilliant sun outside. The jays are singing. He goes up to the bell tower and begins tolling the bell, flinging the clapper again and again until long after he sees them vanish over the last hill, past Chateau, past Sanglier, past Lavoir (where the washerwomen gather), past Fontenay, past Forneau (now clustered with women come to bake their bread), past Avoine, Bonivet (where they turn for their last glimpse of the church), out toward the place names they begin to know as their own, past Sauvegrain, Croix, Villeneuve, Vaugaudry, Benetrie, Aurons, Coldreau, Boutiniere. Here the child wets himself, and as they change the cloth they remark they should rename the place Pissebas—little low-pee—and note to tell him that someday when he is old enough to walk this same road and know his place among its names. Then onward again, past Murier, past Daviderie, where without their entirely realizing it the last of the bells have dwindled to silence.

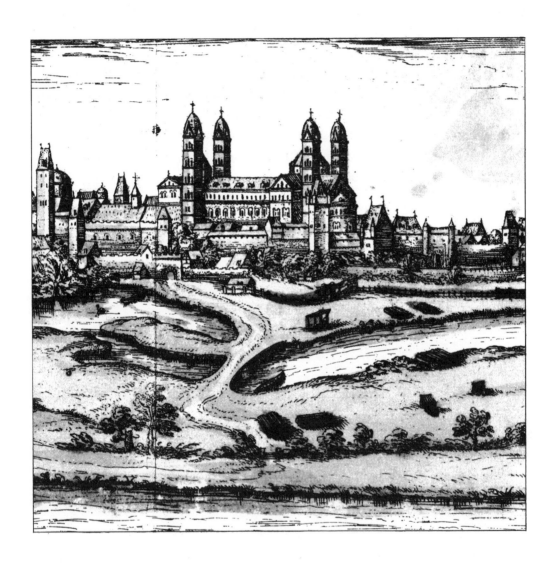

1518

Friarsgate

Out on the road where the town begins, Friar Guillaume begs:

God's cookie, Sire? Bushel of barley, good man, to rest your soul well? Please, Missy, a pretty sou for a mass? . . . Or your mother, perhaps? There! There's your name, down on God's list! A slice of cheese, Sire, if you please? Masses! Rosaries! Trentals! Masses! Rosaries! Trentals!

Begging among workmen, itinerant tinkers, herders, haywards, women balancing loads of laundry, hire horses clopping the hasteless pace of their return to the stable, wet nurses walking with one charge at each breast, urchins holding up baskets of grass for sale, dung collectors carrying empty baskets to the barns and the stables. Carts from the country rumbling on huge wheels.

God's labor for beef and bacon! Into my sack and your prayer's into heaven! We live in poverty. We know no delight. Give us a chicken and you'll be remembered tonight! Prayers for you, kind Sires and Madames, prayers for you speeding to Christ. Our bodies are dead but for our knees and our prayers! Dear people, pay now to God and be paid back in Paradise!

To the river fords, where traffic must slow. Muddy ruts vanish into midstream. A place of thigh-high boots waterproofed with pitch. There the oxen can cross, lolling their heads to each side as they plunge and then wade, the wheels of their wagons groaning axle-deep in the froth. Shepherds look across awaiting a quiet moment, then sizzle to their dogs who begin herding over their flocks. Farmers cross carefully, carrying strapped to their backs a wood-tined new harrow or the mended handles of a plow. A splendidly caped gentleman ferries across on the hire boat, the boatman's lackey leading his shying horse. Urchins besiege the man and he throws the smallest boy a coin, then laughs as the older boys beat him for it.

> God's biscuit, Sire? A coin from your pocket? Almighty Lord bless you, Sire, you'll be remembered tonight. A knock on Purgatory, dear Madame, to send into heaven all your lost children? Into the hat, Madame, whatever you can spare! Prayers to Saint John, good folk, today is his day! A sou for your sister, dear Sir, if she's ailing—or even if she's not! Our prayers will keep her in good health, from hairpiece to slot!

An herb gatherer wades across with his sack, but the lightness of its swing from his belt means he's gotten only fern. Downstream a poacher stoops to pick pebbles, his sling hidden away in a bulge at his waist. Charcoal sellers wade by, forest-fire smells reeking from faces and hands half-skin, half-soot. The smith's hands are huge, beefy, thick fingered; the cooper's have been abraded by a lifetime of slivers. A goose farmer comes across with two huge blankets crammed with feathers. When he clears the town's side, he heads toward the shack of the pillowmaker. Then come two girls, hair high and smiling, arms free of any load, destinations unknown but route noted by every woman they pass.

> We labor for your salvation and can open the Great Door. A chicken, pullet, anything you can give! God saves givers, leaves the others for lost! God's cookie, Sire, a wee God's crust? Into the sack and pray for you we must!

Tolltakers, wagon searchers, quacks selling cremes. A rough shack outside the portal has a wrinkled cloth hanging over two partitions. Inside a physician examines the pustules of a pedlar to see if they are the kind that can spread. A bell hanging from a postern marks the door to the watch's hut at night. He will ring it once a little before sunset, twice as the sun vanishes, and thrice at the last calling of the birds. Then he will unpinion the ropes to two huge chains and the portcullis will grind down to spear into the mud at his feet.

Souls out of Purgatory! Your loved ones freed from their pain! Give what you can. Give what you may. Here, into this book! Devotions for souls you want to be free! Masses! Prayers! Trentals! Masses! Prayers! Trentals! Trentals today—thirty masses for the price of ten. Give what you can, spare not your wealth! Sous in my hat, a God's cookie or piece of meat, and in Heaven your God you'll meet!

Hoop-shaped baskets for winnowing now carry dried flowers. An old man bears a large wooden pot hollowed from a log to a depth greater than his arm's length, which has a mallet-shaped pestle strapped alongside. In the morning he'll wander the town's edges, calling for those who have nuts to press. Once he's mortared them to mash, they can be taken to the public *pressoir* to be pressed until their oil runs free.

A boy hurries past carrying a bundle of skewers for an inn.

Keep your soul sprightly, give your coin lightly! We fast and we pray. We have no bliss. We have no wealth. We are here to bless. We are here to pray. Give, dear Sires and Madames, give what you may. God's ear will hear of you today!

Apprentices, running. A magistrate and gatekeeper rise from their table to examine a cartload of meat, pressing their fingers into the slabs within. Old women carry baskets of dried prunes. A donkey opens its mouth, belches, then wheezes a few gasps into an ascending *hi-han, hi-han, hi-han* that thunders in the tiny passageway beneath the portal.

Toward the end of day Friar Guillaume leaves off from his begging to ponder his gleanings, then pauses a few moments to look over the populace of his gate: minstrels, tinkers, herbsellers, seasonal workers, farmhands, townsmen fleeing town debts, roaming soldiers in search of allegiance, priests headed for marriages and funerals, bishops making the rounds of their parishes before heading to Rome, wandering students, pilgrims with their staffs topped by water gourds, agents of foreign bankers, sellers of chopped snakes and perfume, troupes of actors, beggars, confidence men, sheep and cattle on their way to slaughter, gentry in wagons, hire horses being returned to their stations, oxcarts carrying huge timbers and lead sheets for the roof of a church, merchant convoys with their long trains of wagons and bearded guards, and other friars—begging friars, preaching friars, friars minor, cordeliers, each with his own distinctive habit and manner of begging.

Friar Guillaume is so intent on keeping other friars away from his gate that he scarcely notices a traveler of slight build, drab hat, and muddy boots who is seemingly intent on avoiding the friar's notice, and who is carrying into the town concealed in his boots a sheaf of roughly printed slender pamphlets acclaiming a man in a faraway land speaking a barbarous tongue who has a marvel to tell the world, a man named Luther.

1 5 1 8 : F R I A R S G A T E

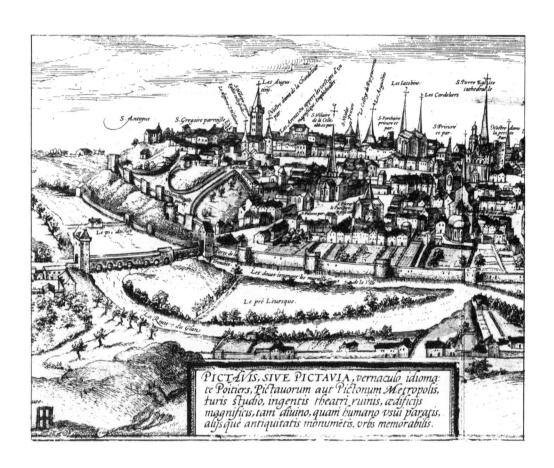

PICTAVIS, SIVE PICTAVIA, vernaculo idioma-
te Poitiers, Pictauorum aut Pictonum Metropolis,
turis studio, ingentis theatri ruinis, ædificijs
magnificis, tam diuino, quam humano vsui paratis,
alijsque antiquitatis monumēris, vrbs memorabilis.

1539

Doomsday for a Market Scribe

The farmers who come to market say, "Who sleeps with his mule at dusk sells first in the morning."

And they come. Toward twilight, dust-laden and tired, they converge from the side paths and tracks. Riding sidesaddle on the backs of their oxen or shuffling along leading their mules, legs steady in their rhythms, prodding along their animals with the tassel-ends of long whips, into Paris's contours of cityscape and populace, they come.

Behind them, incredibly laden animals and carts, almost invisible under burdens of goods to sell, kindling for the fires, pouches of dried fruit, mounds of straw for the animals, baskets woven to pass winter's long nights. Donkeys wheeze beneath sacks brimming with nuts, apples, wheat, greens from creeksides, barrels of back-shed wine. Leather and hemp twines are stretched to their limits.

They pay the fee and enter through the portals. The universities, archbishops, rectors, princes, garrets, garlic peelers, streets, castles, cathedrals, portals, roofs of Paris—these sum to nothing. Paris means marketplace. It has stalls. That is enough.

So they weave unerringly through the labyrinth of streets, heading for the square of the Place de la Bastille, with its tented arcade around the edge. The light is now thinning and they hurry. When they arrive at their familiar stalls, the women make ringlets of stones in which they kindle twig fires. Children blow up the flames until the air froths with sparks. On go basins of water for soups, and thin-hammered pans filled with quickbread doughs, scraps of meat on skewers, mugs to warm the wine, water for washing.

The men unload the hay first to feed the animals. While they are docile, the men's sons hobble their legs to large stones on the ground, then loosen the intricate knots that release their wares. Enormous mushroom-shaped blankets begin to lose their shape as off come the baskets, ristling to the ground in the soft sound of wickerwork. Everything is arranged into a circle to be covered for the night with rush mats and straw, a lumpy but effective bed for the dogs. A dozen chickens cackle together. One pecks out at a passing ankle, jutting its legs backward and revealing that all of them are tied together with a twine of briar runners. The briar still bristles its thorn, no harm to a chicken but a sure deterrent for thieves.

As the animals are unladen the men stroke their backs and check their halters for chafing or bruises. Then their work is done and they look for faces they know. Wineskins begin their gruff rounds in swallows and belches. The low-voiced speech of men used to hard labor rumbles along with curses and guffaws. They stay away from the inns and wineshops, with their fast-talking men and playing cards and shell games and stories too good to be true. They all learned, once.

So mingling together in the kind of talk they alone know, amid the smells and unkemptnesses and things done by necessity, they speak of harvests and weather and times and kings. Silence comes over them as tax collectors arrive on the other side of the square, surrounded by armed guards in crimson and crosses, each on his horse (Horses!—How many barren fields could improve with the help of that strength!), who have arrived to dine with the market officials and to sleep at the inn.

Then to sleep with their wives and children, with cattle, dogs, chickens, dried beans. It is fitful town slumber, disturbed by the shifting of animals and the cry of the watch wandering the streets. A bleary child's eye marks the watch's passage, two or three armed men carrying an flaming oil-soaked rag guttering pale yellow light from the end of a long pole.

· · · · · · · · · ·

The first arrivals in the morning look deformed in the shadowy murk of predawn. Then from shoulder slings and waist bags spill bundles and baskets. Into this one goes a mound of dried grapes, into that one peas; a third cradles newly washed eggs. A woman unrolls a cloth which was spindled around her waist and mats it down flat, revealing dozens of patties of fresh butter, each on its own leaf still moist from the night's chill.

Tinkers set out tiny anvils and knee-squeezed bellows made of sewn leather. One surrounds himself with hammers and tongs, pancakes of rude tin, puddles of lead, a charcoal brazier on which he precedes everything with a breakfast of minced meat in a pie.

Next to him, and wrinkling his nose at the smell of hot metal, the market scribe Eustache Lefief pins on the badge of his trade: a feather in his hat. A document maker by training and a poet by claim, Eustache can write in Latin and all the local dialects with a hand that is upright and fluid, servicable enough for betrothal pacts and tradesmen's contracts—but not for the bishop's chancery.

Unknown even to himself, Eustache is the most lettered of all the Lefiefs. Being the eleventh of fifteen children, there was at his birth no hope of land or goods. The family patrimony by then had been spread so thin that his parents, Arnoul and Plaisance, gave him at the age of his maturity, twelve, a choice between the clergy or the military. But as luck would have it, there was an appointment open for a commoner as apprentice copyist in the chancery of the Bishop of Toul. Eustache began in 1498 what he presumed to be a long and comfortable, if tedious, life reproducing wills, testaments, citations of canon law, the squabbles of clerics, records of baptisms and confirmations, procedural agreements between local lords and the bishopric.

Sadly, due to a minor defect of birth, his writing hand was misshapen. Though his script was legible, his manner of holding a quill alarmed the other copyists, and after twenty-two years of training and service, he was denied vows. In 1520, at the age of thirty-four and with only his penmanship to support him,

71

he headed unerringly for the one place he knew he would be able to provide for himself a subsistence: Paris.

Now at the age of fifty-three, in moderate health and possession of most of his teeth, he salves his pride by maintaining to clients that, yes, a chancery clerk has a fine hand, but after all is not such a clerk reduced to a mere copyist who must have no sense of design of his own? Why, what chancery clerk would ever dare illuminate his script?

Eustache concludes these thoughts as he thins his ink in a thimbleful of water. Life is better here in the market, he tells himself. Does he not know nearly everyone by first name and next of kin? What could possibly replace that as the goal of a life's vocation? Paper knowledge, he maintains, tends to fill books and empty heads, while people knowledge tends to do the opposite. Why, in this very city of Paris, does not the faculty of the University expel those who work with their hands? Unhandy minds and unminded hands—where have these led if not to lives ruled by habit first, fear second, and rumor third? Doesn't he alone, with his scripts and paper and penmanship and ink, possess the power to move people, to bring them to that which they otherwise would not believe? To everyone else in the market, should they think so far, the past is nostalgia, the present survival, the future so colored by soothsayers that it resembles the sun after passing through the stained windows of the church. No, the scribe sees these illusions for what they are, for is he not similarly able to create images from ink-tints and verbs?

So he sets out his tools: a hardwood easel with three legs, dozens of quills with tufts of feather each of a special feel so he can pick one out without having to glance up from his work, a scraper to work away dried ink, small cups to thin inks so a rewritten document can be matched to the original, a dozen thumbnail-sized crucibles for blending pigments, twigs to mix water dipped from a boxwood mug.

Eustache looks up. The detail of market life parades before his eyes. Loops of leather sewn into tunics belie the handles of workers' tools and thus the signs of their trades: the shearers and shapers and fine knives of leather workers and shoemakers; for the goldsmith tiny hammers and pliers; for the horse hobbler large loops for rope and small ones for nails; for the market watch sturdy back leather for rings with dozens of keys; for the cheese seller two huge pouches for loaves and thin slits for dull knives.

In an unclaimed corner a forester lays down stacks of twigs for those who need fire. Next to him lie heaps of lentils spilled over a sack's brim, sprays of parsley tied in bunches, urns of fresh milk circling a mound of fresh cheese— soft, white cheese, riven by crevices after being loosened from its cloth. The stallholder picks away grass bits, shakes away the last watery whey, and with a little patterned wood pommel stamps her design in its middle. The design, reversed and indented, is a cross and a flower, carved by her husband on a wintry fireside night.

One of the men now wraps some straw around the horns of a heifer, the sign that she's for sale. She is small and thin hipped. No one inquires about the look in his eyes as he calls out her virtues, but he's got the accent of the province next door, owned by a marquis who believes kingdom is as simple as the felicity of the fate that gave him his station, and that if his land is half as peopled it thus must be twiced as taxed. Why else would such a fine animal need be sold this time of year?

Amid her gentle lowings there rise the tents, draped on poles held fast by piles of stones. Burlap roofs flurry dust as they go up. A well-dressed drunk man wrestles with a laundress near the square's fountain, but her entreaties for help bring no one for no one dares challenge wealth. And besides, what true laundress would be so naive as to wear a low blouse? A chestnut seller is stolid next to their scuffle, tending to her fire and blackened pans with puffy fingers and thick arms, silent to the cries next to her.

A man arrives with a dripping basket. He finds a small place for himself near the fountain, gets a bucket of water, splashes it over the basket, then opens it. A small army of snails begins a tentative escape. He tosses the speed-kings back into the bottom of the bucket. Tiny antennae unfurl again and ponder their way forward.

An eggseller arrives, wearing his tradesman's signature of an old straw hat and a rolled-up pouch containing his product and his coin. He carries a wicker basket filled with chickens and straw. The chickens go into a pile in the center, tied by their ankles. The rooster of the lot manages to raise himself valiantly from the dust to crow a hoarse protest, stepping on and being pecked by the hens in the process. He is halfway through a magnificent *cocorico* when a boy on a passing mule cart tosses a pile of hay on him.

Then a clothseller commences her *cri*:

> What do ye lack, what do ye buy?
> See what ye lack, see with ye eye!
> Pins and points and ribbons and garters,
> Lace from Spain and feather-trimmed darters!

She marks out her wares in rhythm and rhyme—amencloth in double twill; bombassin and brusselcloth and bustyans from Flanders; chamblette and cogware both available in crimson; durance and damask and dowlas from Denmark; estamine and frisadue and gallonier with grosgraine; janet with horsehair and kersey without; linsey-woolsey woven in blue; pampilion and passamayne and penniston from England at thirty-seven ells to the length, riggscloth, russelcloth, sarcene, and satin; taffeta with spangles and tilsent without—her cries echoed by the pieseller next door:

> Hot pippin pies, hot hot hot!
> Hot pudding pies, hot hot hot!
> Hot suet pies, hot apple pies, all of them hot!
> All of them all of them hot hot hot!

Then the professionals, the leathermakers, harness repairers, plowmakers, toothpullers, weavers, fortunetellers, dispensers of salt, storytellers, barrelmakers:

> Have ye wood to sell, good good wood?
> A cooper I am and hoopin's my trade.
> I've got the best little wife
> God ever made!

A farmer alludes to the secret of his *prunelle*: soak a measure of prunes in five measures of wine, add honey, stir, let marry for two days, drain, and . . .

> Friste, freste, prune wine's the best!
> Cric, crac, how much do ye lack?
> Ziste, zeste, it's wine to digest!
> Piffe, paffe, you'll crap up a stack!

He passes out a taste of it so potential customers can gauge for themselves. Then, appetite sharpened by his own claims, he takes time out for a simple meal of snails and acorns, washed down with goat's milk and wine.

A traveling butcher sets up the sign of his trade, the skull of a cow spread across the roofbeam of his tent. A mendicant friar passes his bowl, singing:

> Masses, rosaries, trentals!
> Rosaries for your loved ones and old ones too!
> Trentals, Trentals, Trentals today!
> Thirty masses without cease for those in Purgatory's retreat!

The silversmith across from Eustache sets out his tools: dozens of pawls, all wide-handled to fit his palm. A varied assortment of point styles from diamond-shaped with sharp edges for plowing a smooth furrow to blunt tips for smoothing out waves and wrinkles, slender hammers with various sizes of peen, a rabbit's foot with soft hair for polishing to a sheen, cotter's pincers to pick up fine wires, a small anvil with one end round and the other a point, dividers and small vises, rough bars of raw metal, rasps, burring tools, soft cloths, and a work table of smoothed marble.

Nearby a stallboy works in tattered boots and cast-off clothes, sweating as his wooden spade scrapes up knee-deep piles of urine and filth, his face biliously yellow from hundreds of animals.

Then Eustache spots something he cannot recall having seen before. A man arrives nearby with a pack on his back scarcely larger than his chest, whose contents he lays out in several rows—wares so unusual as to be virtually an apparition: chapbooks covered with blue paper, each containing a two dozen or more identical pages. Eustache, being a man whose marks on paper convey other people's meanings, knows the importance of graven words as well as he knows the importance of baptism.

But the literature of the marketplace has always before been crude—improbable deeds by saints and knights or anticlerical tomfooleries disguised as skits, all of them impressed from carved wooden blocks by papermakers of poor skill, smudged with ink from print blocks being slid away carelessly at an angle, smeared from the thumbprints of a pass-along readership of thousands, fading to one side or another from a poorly inked press, and moved roughly from toll station to toll station by itinerant friars and renegade monks. The chapbook's chunky depictions and inelegant text has been the way the marketsquare populace has learned of kingdoms, heroes, legends, foreigners.

But these, Eustache shakes his head, these are so very *different*! He discerns immediately the improvements in quality. Far from the crude, rough-edged images and oversize letters of the woodcuts of his time, these pages are as if graven in silver. He fetches over the silversmith to get an expert opinion. The smith nods and says, yes, this is of the quality of fine worked silver—see how the lines in the pictures are combined equally of broad and thin, see how the metal's surface has been stippled by fine burins to create the dotwork of clouds, see how the maker has worked a series of fine parallel lines into the illusion of cloth—yes, the smith nods, this picture cannot have been made but from silver. But then he shakes his head—no, silver cannot be pressed unto paper for paper is too strong, silver loses its edge, silver bends under pressure, silver is altogether too soft for this kind of impression.

And yet there are so many! *Dozens* with the same title! Why, everyone knows woodblock chapbooks are so laborious they can be made only one at a time! Doesn't every tradesman carry but one copy of each work? What manner of commerce is this when a seller travels alone with no donkey and carries dozens of the same title?

They turn to the seller, who shrugs his shoulders, and relates how he picked them up at a very advantageous price from a workshop in Lyons of whom none of them had ever heard, that of one Claude Nourry. And the name of this work! What could one possibly make of the title *Les horribles et espoventables faictz a prouesses du tresrenome Pantagruel Roy des Dipsodes*?

The chapbook seller, under the pressure of what he takes to be a hostile reception, lets slips four words which they have all heard but which none recognizes as a sea wave of change rising far beyond the shoreline's eye: "graven copper" and "moveable letters."

. . . .

The market is divided into *quartiers*. One is for food and spices, another for animals and hay and leather, a third for implements and smiths and labor. Another is the most colorful of all—bolts of cloth, rows of wooden spoons, women crushing cardamoms.

Daughters stand there, their waist-length hair hanging loosely in a fan. Every eye present knows they're soon to be wed, for beautiful hair on a new wife who must now work is of no use. Fingers press, comb, twist, appraise. One girl is in tears, betrothed to a higher born who on her own she would never touch, but from whom she must now bear numberless children, her life now extinct but for the conceiving, feeding, cleaning, teaching, dying, all for a merchant no one but her mother could love. Her mother pinches her elbow and describes to a customer the hairpiece that could be fashioned from such tresses.

A section amid these is set aside for dealers in discards. Used cloaks, torn cloth, strips of leather from the trash of a shoemaker, piles of cloth destined for rags, potions, amulets, scented candles, rosaries of strung beans. Money-changers weigh their used coins, old men with tight lips and tight purses and tiny balances under the Sign of the Scales. Palm-kneading Gypsy women in brilliant costumes with jewels stroke hands with their long fingers and sing the roundelay:

Almanac, almanac, fine fine almanac!
Fine fine almanac the rest of the year!
The rest of the year you'll find it all here!
You'll find it all here, almanac, almanac!

A seller of sweet scents stands amid his pouches of powders, woods from far shores, thick substances gummy with camphor, bay leaves, flower blossoms, dozens of seeds, expensive pigments in carved wooden boxes. As the day warms he grooms his stall, then starts a small fire. When it dies into coals he takes up a pinch of tiny purple petals and sprinkles them onto the coals, which then erupt into lavender. He does it again and the smoke billows high and the sellers of used clothes crowd around his advertisement-cum-fumigation. They display their wares by hanging them over their outstretched arms like great woolen-winged angels.

Toothpullers sit under open-sided tents, buckets of water alongside. In a pouch hanging from a peg are their tongs, pliers, knives, scrapers, and strips of cloth to wad into the hole.

An apothecary sets up some planks on sawhorses, drooping a tattered cloth over the front. Out come bags, bottles, painted cards, sacks, trays, bins, ladles, phials stoppered with twigs, bits from a cadaver dried in the sun, hedgehog quills by the hundredweight, powdered mushrooms, dead green beetles, dried flowers, thick gums. Slivers of rare woods, the dried skins of hedgehogs turned spiny side in. Lizard tails, shells tied together with string, broken bird wings, dried blood, silvery dusts, the boiled-down fat of a felon hung outside of a churchyard.

The apothecary knows his timing as well as his words. First a quick babble as he sets up his stall, then a low drone as down go his baskets. A reverential silence as he puts up a crucifix, then a low muttered prayer as he unrolls a wood-cut of the Virgin. The morning crowds don't buy, they're all old women and paupers. Toward midday he holds up a phial and begins to sell in earnest:

. . . and if you fail to be fixed, may my ventpeg slip, my stopper fail me, my poop-pipe collapse, and my fundament fall out! Is there any man or woman among you to say that it's contrary to law or faith, against any reason, not self-evident, or opposed to Divine Writ? No! Far from it! There's not a word in the Holy Book that stands against it! I ask you, look back on your days and try to count the number of times you've had coughing spells, sweating states, sneezing attacks, hiccups that won't stop, bad breath, farts with or without sound, hemorrhages, ague, bad sleep, bad dreams, bad eliminations, the rash, attacks of tears, paroxysms at any hour, mucus from your nose, hemorrhoids, or spells of the wheeze! If so, God's good merciful name be praised! He has turned your feet to me today! For who among you will tell me it cannot be true? Ha-haaa! May I drop dead on the spot if a single word I say is a freewilliger lie! Made from a secret formula by the mystic apothecaries of Galore, it contains exotic dried roots, fruits, leaves, berries, gums, seeds, barks, and juices. There's not a wisewoman alive who wouldn't churn it, whirl it, jumble it, tumble it, stroke it, beat it, bump it, tweak it, bang it, shake it, lift it, clip it, eye it, smell it, breathe it in, look at it twice and breathe it back out, fondle it, splash it, whiff it, stuff it, swig it, savor it, sip it, relish it, enjoy it, smack her lips at it, belch twice, and declare it ambifanfreluchelatedly good for oils and boils, breaks and shakes, quivers and shivers, colds and molds, sneezes and wheezes, sweats that wet, cases of bile, and attacks of catarrh! There isn't a piddle, poop, sob, sneeze, cough, yawn, snore, sweat, hack, hawk, bark, whoop, snort, snivel, snuff, mewl, weep, twit, howl, yowl, wiggle, or waggle that won't throw up its hands and head for the rear door! Sharp nose, sunken eyes, hollow temples, cold ears, tight forehead, hurting gums, wrinkled eyelids, blue veins, and soussulated teeth! Gone, ladies and gentlemen, gone, gone, GONE!

. . . .

Day moves across market like summer across fruit, from richness to ripeness to rot. Afternoon brings clots of flies and scavengers and pickers of spoils. A prostitute walks by, exhausted from births, nursing a child from her wrinkled breast.

79

Snatches of work sounds ring out from the stalls. A donkey sneezes, rasp to wheeze to cough to thunderclap. A woodcutter's saw shreds through a plank, the wood's hollow gnash descending from splinter to clatter. Muleteers go *Shyaaahh!* Two chatterbox fast-talkers are too distant for anything but their insistence to be heard. Beneath these sounds lies the labyrinth of the marketsquare's countertenor: cat's hiss, boy squabbles, pig's squeal, mule wheezes, anvil's ring, the scent seller's newest explosion. A woman on an errand hurries by with her newborn, the infant bound in linen and slung over her back, head lolling as it sleeps to her song.

An old carpenter's bucksaw still does a straight line, even though now in his dotage he has to plane his work to make its edges smooth. His stall is poised eternally on collapse. Its only light comes from a single hole in the roof. Sunshafts illumine the interior's dusts, the skitter of cedar chips arcing across the floor, the pee-mound of chips in a far corner. Sitting on one of his freshly sawn stumps, he talks with a customer as he holds a dovetail between his hands and his knee. The smell of wood is everywhere. He barks an order at his son, whose momentary duty is to keep the dust down with water fetched from the well.

A few men dislodge from their work and seek out a tattered sign hanging from a pole in front of a shop. It is a painted cloth banner with the fading image of a grinning pop-eyed fish in bright red on a dark green background. Rough print announces, "The Fried Carp Inn." From behind the thick canvas door there comes the unmistakable smoke-and-wine-dregs smell of a drinking place.

Inside, the inn is smoky, dim, lighted only by guttering fish-oil lamps which sting the eyes until they begin to adjust. Then the new arrivals can make out the shapes of a dozen or more men, most of them seated on long benches or at rough-hewn tables, with a few others standing at a bar of flat boards. Behind the bar is an enormous bristle-bearded man with a rag around his neck and a wine pot in his hand. He fills it from one of the large *tonnes* on wood cradles stacked to the ceiling. His is blunt wine for blunt men: *rouge, rouge,* and *rouge,* five or seven deniers the measure, depending on whether it is accompanied by a herring.

The ceiling is so black with soot that only some dangling spiderwebs confirm a ceiling to be there. The men at the tables sit on three-legged stools, leaning forward and shouting into each other's faces. Each has his own bib, a piece of matted wool that combines as a napkin, sweat rag, and horse curry. The roar of talk and laughter suffocates all other senses. A man bawls something to the innkeeper's daughter, who is sitting at a fire grilling halved herrings. They spatter and crackle greasy smoke clouds out into the room. Another man wipes off his mouth with the back of his hand as he sets down a tankard. He stops a narrative in midsentence, temporarily distracted by a fish bone in a tooth, which he tries to dislodge with a knife. Others are roasting plucked songbirds, then eating them drumstick by tiny drumstick. Under the tables several dogs have established a hierarchy of the bone piles. In one corner is a ladder with two missing rungs. It ascends perilously to a shelf of earthenware crocks, dust-covered bottles, a funnel made from a gourd, and jugs shaped from boiled leather. A cat curls there sleeping, its tail tip just covering its nose.

Around the beam posts are pegs on which men have flung their hats. Most are the plain felt hats of workingmen—a smith's hat of dark blue with a low brim, a beggar's hat with a thick rolled-up edge to make it easy to hold, a drover's hat shaped like a helmet to keep off the rain. A student's hat seems incongruous in bright red with a feather.

Two men at the tables wear the rough wool and leather chaps of *debardeurs*, haulers of heavy goods who own their teams of oxen. Their jackets are stained and frayed, with bramble snags and twig punctures. One of them lays his coiled whip on a table covered with fish spines and herring heads. He wipes his hand across his mouth and bellows for wine in a voice like the last moments of a bull.

. . . .

As the afternoon dust slowly invades, prices begin to fall. The bargain hunters shuffle into action—the poor, the landless, the beggars with leaking eyes or amputated arms. It is the time of the sun's thinning and the afternoon's broken fruit.

81

Brooms brooms!
Good brooms old, good brooms new!
Busking for brooms,
and old boots too!

Rats 'n' mice! Rats 'n' mice!
Polecats 'n' weasels, sows with measles!
Kill them all what peeps from holes!
Good good poison for creepers 'n' peepers!

A drifting snatch thief feasts his fingers on the tumult. He wears a long cloak
and carries a crooked stick. He flourishes on the disturbances and dogfights,
aiming at the attention-diverting argument that loosens eyes from their wares,
the drunk squabble between two ox-handlers or the goat that's eaten through
its rope and now leads its owners on a winding chase. The soprano of a pig being
carried by one ear and its tail is diversion enough for his hooked stick to rake
in a lettuce. An insult exchange between two harridans culminates in a cantata
of shrieks so elaborate the entire market cranes a free ear—and the scavenger's
sleeve nets two eggs, a sprig of parsley, and a quick three swallows of wine from
an unattended mug. And having long since learned the value of patience, he waits
innocently nearby until the negligent owner returns to hoist the mug. As a dark
look comes over his face and he upbraids his neighbor he loses two apples and
a bunch of grapes for his efforts. A flurry of yells and running feet signal something stolen by another thief. As the thief weaves a serpentine ring ending in
a dust-punctuated fight, the scavenger nets a cuff load of cheeses. The struggle
of two hobbled sheep results in two eggs and a prune. He pauses every few
minutes to ponder his gleanings, eat what he can, then store the rest in a burlap
bag off in the parking lot of the donkeys.

Quick, quick, mussels, quick!
Eels, eels, fine young eels!
Cockles cockles, great cockles great!
And plaice, plaice, fine fat plaice!

Good for your gullet,
Good for your gout!
Oil for your gut,
Within and without!

Out on the periphery, standing amid their stick-supported roofs and canvas awn-
ings and faded cloth banners, guildsmen work with their sons. Smiths, roofers,
tanners, silversmiths, carpenters, weavers, potters, bakers, upholsterers, tinsmiths,
braziers, plank sawyers, shoemenders, embroiderers.

The details of trades first shaped Paris: The sheep grew wool, the shepherd guarded it, the shepherdess cut and washed and combed it, the shepherd's
son took it to market, the parter bought and sorted it, the dyer tinted it, the
oiler sprinkled it with oil, the mixer rubbed the oil in, the carder made patties
of it, the spinster spun it, the weaver made cloth of it, the brayer cleaned the
cloth of dirt and burrs, the burler removed knots and loose ends, the fuller washed
it, the walker tromped it while still in the bath, the shearman turned it and leveled
its nap, the drawer stretched it until it was finished, then the merchant sold it
and the housewife bought it. Once bought the wife's daughters cut it, the maid
trimmed it, the embroiderer decorated it, the seamstress finished it, and the husband paid for it.

Yet this is but the beginning of the details of the trades. In one corner of
the square, two felters make blankets for horses. In front of their stall are huge
baskets filled with wet wool. It is clumpy, wet, matted, filled with briar. The
youngest sons tend glumly to carding and cleaning, taking up tufts and swashing
them between two bristled combs, this way and that, turning the wool again
and again until it is fluffy and clean enough to be taken to the troughs and be
washed. Then it is carded once again until it is smooth.

Beside the two men are baskets filled with now-clean fleece. The men's
wives shape it into palm-sized, wispy-edged flat patties. The younger of the two
men carefully arranges these into a large rectangular shape, overlapping the pieces,
squaring the edges, piling them five to six deep. His brother begins tamping them
with a wood switch, lightly at first, then harder. When the fluffy edges begin

to mingle into a mat, he slips on wooden shoes and starts treading on the mat. He walks doubly around the periphery, then sideways, up and down, back and forth, until the mat has become blanketlike and dense enough to be lifted. The two of them lift it onto a sturdy wooden table, then wet it with water, dye, and soaps. The soap froths thickly and penetrates into the fibers. Then the men's shoulders knot and their backs stiffen as they bend into the most exacting part of their trade: kneading the fibers into a oneness that will not fray. Foam and color squeeze up between their fingers and they begin to sweat even though the day is cool. From nones until vespers they sweat over one blanket, sometimes walking on the mat, then going back to kneading, their feet and hands becoming the color of the day.

Then to the trough, carrying the rolled-up blanket dripping between them. There they wash and rinse it a dozen or more times until the water runs clear. They take it back to the wooden table, which their sons have cleaned and washed while they were gone, and check both sides of the blanket to get rid of any last imperfections. Then a discarded door weighted with large stones goes on top to flatten it. At dusk they will lift away the stones and hang the new blanket over the cross beam that holds up their roof to dry overnight. The sides of their shop are lined with piles of their week's work. Brushed and trimmed, the blankets are folded three or four together in a rainbow of colors.

Afternoon comes in wind puffs and a breeze, wafting char smells from the braziers toward the tied-up dogs, who add a fanfare of howls to the donkey wheezes and haggling.

Garlic, garlic, good good garlic!
Good garlic young and good garlic tart!
Garlic, garlic, fine young garlic!
Garlic, garlic, to make you fart!

The afternoon sun's thinning turns thoughts to the long trip home. Boys braising meat enjoy a huge trade. Their charcoal-heaped pans are stacked full across with meats on iron skewers: chunks of goat marinated two days in cumin and wine, fatty chopped pork rolled expertly into sausages, bits of beef skewered on sticks. Smoke roils upward, agonizing the dogs.

Around, the pace thins. Melons and cabbages are slung into nets, broken cauliflowers and green peppers go for a song. Girls with water jars teeter along carefully, puffs of dust scooting back from their feet. Boys stop chasing each other only to taunt cripples. Fathers' orders bring groans. Visits are made to the fuel sellers' stalls, the reeking premises of charcoal makers with black faces, black hands, black mules, who pride themselves on never washing. The straw mats that were last night's mattresses are now taken down from the day's airing in the sun and rolled into tubes. A mule, freed from its rope harness for a moment, immediately kneels and flops on its side to roll deliciously in the dirt.

A leatherware seller begins to disassemble his ornate and incredibly complicated display. First off come the low things, the purses and portfolios for papers and coins, the hats, tooled fringework, ankle chaps for shepherds, thin leather for shoes and thick leather for soles, thongs for laced bodices. Following them come the egg baskets, lawyers' satchels, shallow panniers, magnificently patterned sheaths for documents and ledgers, pieces of fine red-brown leather from Cordoba to make into jacket cuffs or collars.

All these come loose as if by magic. When he begins to reach for the topmost items, the slow sellers like jackets and table coverings, he takes up a slim hooked stick, deftly reaches up, loosens the desired item without disturbing its neighbors, and lifts it easily away without collapsing the entire construction. His deftness mystifies a handful of snatch thieves, who have been hovering nearby for hours, trying to discern the stealable items in that honeycomb of straps, handles, hooks, and pegs. They realize they've been defeated and shuffle off. The leather seller sees this without acknowledging them and relaxes his vigilance. A long stretch up to the topmost item, spare straps for a harness, then that's gone too.

Heaps of grain and dried beans vanish into aprons and shawls. Reluctant mules accept their wooden saddles shaped like trestles. One of them doesn't and starts kicking. Everyone scatters and laughs and it is kicked and pulled by the tail until it regrets having even breathed, and the saddle goes on uneventfully.

Dogs are untied and their recently established harmony dissolves into growls and fights. Wandering youths follow girls, jogging each other and smirking. Younger boys trail the youths and listen avidly as the youths speak grandly of Lyons and Tours and other places they haven't been—the nights with the girls there, the delights, the sighs. Their faces are crestfallen as they are interrupted by commands from their fathers.

Eustache the scribe looks up from his work for the first time today. All these hours he has worked on a baptismal certificate, curling flowery lines to every corner of the page, then filling them with names and dates and brief sketches from the lives of saints. He knows his place on that page, the smiling artificer peering from the lacework of the first letter of the first word, just as God painted Himself into the first word of Genesis. Has not art depicted itself always thus, a face smiling into the immensity of things?

Yet now that he looks around Eustache notices the chapbook seller has gone. Odd, he thinks. Who would leave the marketplace until the day was over? He asks his neighbors whatever has become of the fellow. They reply that his booklets were sold long before noon, so he returned to Lyons to pick up some more. Two stallholders proudly display the copies they bought for themselves, a marketplace ribaldry so hilarious it has made their day.

. . . .

A fruitseller consults with his wife. She departs. He begins by releasing the dozens of knots that keep aloft their sackcloth sunshade. It crumples in a tangle on top of their wares, gusting clouds of flies out from the edges. He pulls free the loops from half a dozen pegs, and his tent falls in on itself with a great clatter. He gathers the ropes, winding each between his elbow and palm, giving each skein a half-twist so it loops into a figure eight.

His wife returns with their sad-eyed donkey. They fold their burlap sacks into two pouched bags, knot them in several places, then throw them over the donkey's back. These they fill with their unsold melons, apples, grapes, milk, lentils. Wicker hampers take in the week's purchases, over which the woman has bartered for half the day.

They relate to each other the times when they wouldn't see specie or coin for a month. But those times seem to be gone. A good king has changed the face of the marketplace. The stallholder and his wife haven't decided what to make of it. Coin gets things done more quickly, but they miss the old chats. The roads are now free of robbers, so their eldest sons can work the fields rather than working their swords, but how odd that these sons seem uninterested in the girls of their hamlet. Everyone sees neighbors less, having little to say in the absence of barter. There are more goods, some from far away, but everything seems expensive and becoming more so. Life is less dangerous, but there are more frauds. There is more of everything, but such quantities seem made for something larger than the marketsquare they know.

Scratching his head, Eustache tries to divine the meaning of these things. The use of this new thing called print is already closing off monasteries to book copying, and now Eustache foresees a flood of the very chapbooks he saw today. He is no fool. He realized their importance the moment he saw how readable they were. But what frightens him suddenly is the speed of their selling. What— oh *dares* he ask?—what would it mean to the substance of his life if there came to the marketplace a trader of baptismal certificates, wedding announcements, encouragements to enter an order, bequeathals of small holdings too negligible for the attention of a priest?

No, Eustache assures himself. That could not be. How could printed pieces of paper possibly replace his scribe's erudition? What fool would prefer the gracelessness of fixed phrases to the erudition and attention of his time?

That he cannot imagine. He has not yet heard of the word "nouvelles," now being used for the first time to describe events of unprecedented origin, literally "news." That "news," too, has begun to be conveyed in print would utterly mystify him. No, the beauty of the old way, the beauty of things as they are, the spirit of the market and its people—these are life, and life, given by God, can never change. What could possibly change the Place de la Bastille?

Of a man named Luther and his squabbles with the Church, of these Eustache has of course heard but takes to be of no more import than the squabbles between friars. Of the King's court and his drawing of courtiers under the jewels of one crown, of these Eustache knows but little. Of a new and growing class of merchants who buy and sell coin instead of things and who take their wisdom from books rather than the marketplace, of these he knows next to nothing. Of the gold now coming from some land called America and of its silently cheapening everyone's currencies, of this he is entirely ignorant. And of the immense wave that will engulf forever the lives of his great-great-great-great-great-great grandchildren in this very square a quarter of a millennium hence, it is an invisible tremor so far out to sea no one even suspects its existence.

The fruitseller and his wife now finish their day. Straw mats and coarse blankets are rolled up and tied to the donkey's flanks. Two urns of milk, sealed by leather circlets tied with cord, go into nets hung over the saddle. Wads of hay in coarse nets hang on the donkey's neck, unused fodder to be taken home. When the donkey begins to shuffle and tread uneasily, the man calms it with a pat and a mumble, puts on a few last things, then turns to his wife.

She picks up a net, loops it over her shoulders, then bends forward to balance the load of shawls, homespun blankets to keep them warm after twilight, figure eights of rope, a new pair of sandals, a tiny pouch of pepper, a bit of marzipan for Grandma, three pots, the charcoal brazier for cooking supper, the sootgreasy grill, and cloth spindles containing the food they will nibble on the way home. Finding no convenient place for their earthen cooking pot, she puts it over her head, tilting it just enough so she can see the ground.

She stands. Her husband adjusts the net's leather headband as she leans into it, loops her fingers through the cords, balances the load, and finds the angle she will maintain for the next seven hours. He ties the donkey's cord to his waist, picks up a cloth bag of fruit in each hand, and adjusts his hat with his wrist.

They move forward as one. The clamor of Paris, of children and dogs and drovers and churchbells and archbishops and perfumers and artists and lawyers dwindles in intensity but is still faintly audible an hour out into the silence.

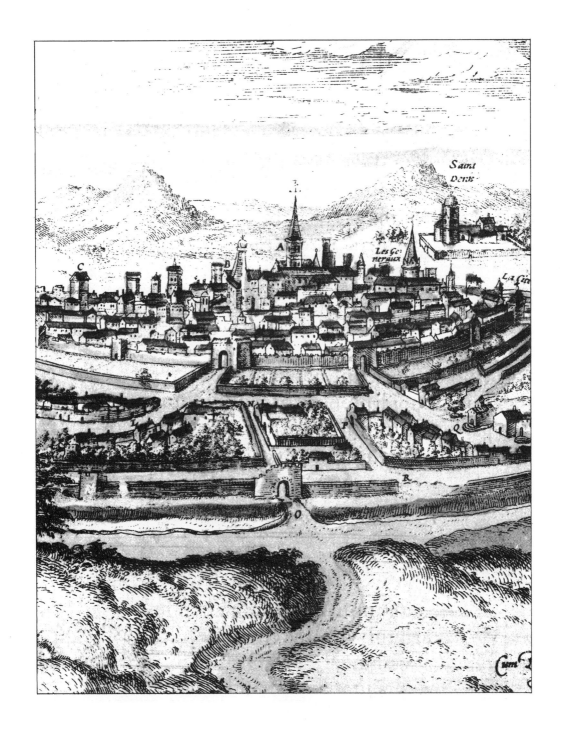

1603

A Donkey Is Sold at Nimes

Guy Lefief, the donkey seller, arrives early. Before dawn, a ghost on the path, eyes gritty from cold and short sleep, riding atop his best animal, tugging along the other donkey which today he hopes to sell. Already he has decided—indeed, long since decided—on the price he will ask, the price he will accept, the price he would like to get, and the price beneath which he will be on this same path within half a day's time, the donkey trailing behind, recipient of ten thousand curses. Guy rides with his friends, the handful of villagers he trusts to do the real selling. Only the others talk, and only about everything which may be seen at the market at Nimes except the dozens of other donkeys which will be for sale there.

Guy cannot conceal his glances at the animal behind him. When weeks ago he and the other villagers realized this donkey was the only item in common among them which could be sold to satisfy the demands of a Crown immersed in yet another war, the donkey was then a sturdy animal, fine-flanked, young, good in health, unaggressive, broad-hooved. Glorious were the prices they imagined that day under the silvery light of the churchyard oak. They passed a wineskin and congratulated each other on their astute bargaining. But now it *is* today, and perhaps the donkey's gait is not as it should be and the animal has been biting lately—which it never did before. But how to explain these sudden

91

and temporary aberrations of choler to a buyer who likewise owes an impost to the Crown and who thus must conceal every sou?

No, it would be foolish to try, so one must hope that their animal, conditioned to life in a hamlet, will not be terrified by the notorious aggressiveness of town donkeys which bite and spit and belch. Guy now prays fervently that when he turns the donkey into the herd the others will eat their grass quietly and not turn their backsides to it, a donkey gesture of contempt. For Guy knows that everything his animal does will be seen, evaluated, and each defect, no matter how temporary, deducted from his price.

His mind rehearses yet again his version of the animal's history. The chafed sores he will explain away as a minor incident while being broken to the harness. The lame knee (now almost fully healed!) from stepping into a badger hole at plowing time. But the subtler signs of intestinal complications and unexpurged parasites which only he, among the sellers, buyers, go-betweens, advisors, inspection agents, shepherds, and village authorities, only he knows for their true extent—these from this hour simply do not exist.

They arrive near dawn and head for a walled square pungent with centuries of donkey smell. The light is pale, thin, sand colored. Guy glances hopefully one last time at his donkey, relieved that it moves comfortably even as it is led among the others. Guy's friends hobble the animal and bind it tail to nose with the others, for donkeys are most comfortable amid the familiar smells of one another's urine, each with its distinct odor of fodder and watering places. Guy breathes a sigh of happiness—his assigned place is near the center of the market where the first buyers will come.

The buyers, on the other hand, have breakfasted well and risen late—just in time for predawn matins. Last night they celebrated a fine repast of chicken and wine, which the seller ruminates upon as he recalls his last evening's village repast of boiled turnips and lentils, concluding that the buyers' meal was paid for with some of the money they might have spent on the donkeys they have come to bargain for; thus they have already cheapened his animal. The parley between buyer and seller has even now begun.

The buyers and their friends talk of little else than donkeys as they walk to the market. Donkeys they do own, donkeys they did own, donkeys they sold for good prices, donkeys they wish they could have owned, donkey lineages, donkey lame spots, donkey sicknesses and donkey health, what a donkey's cloudy eyes might mean, how to hobble a wild donkey, what must be done if a mother's milk is bad or her teats run dry.

They speak of varying donkey prices from market to market, what to deduct for every known malady, how to spot a bad biter even if it is quiet, what to offer, when to offer it, and to whom to offer it. The buyers alone speak of these things, for as buyers such is their right. The others offer suggestions but the buyers' word is final. These others, however, speak louder than the buyers, for it is their voices the buyers wish the sellers to hear—loud, ominous, raucous voices, voices seemingly everywhere around them, voices which make the eyes of a seller stare at the ground, scrutinize mountains far in the distance, blink quickly or stare impassively while a flurry of confusing offers whirls as dispiriting and headache-bringing as the Nimes mistral wind.

When the buyers arrive they disperse and walk among the tethered animals, mendicant friars, bread sellers, crowds of boys. The dust is thick with almond-colored light and the air trembles with donkey bellows, hollering hawkers of fruit, itinerant storytellers, the mournful squalling of jays.

Off to one side there is a corral, many young boys, and a cardsharp's stall surrounded by spectators. The buyers don't glance here; this is the parking lot. As people wander in the clouds of dust and noise, they see friends they sometimes haven't heard about in years. They smile and shake hands, the air filled with the remembrances of mutual friends. Many do not come here to buy but merely to see, and among them are the sham buyers who delight in driving empty bargains. But these can be driven only so far before they are unmasked: all the seller need do is demand a go-between, who, once his hand is shaken, sees a sale to conclusion—and whomever refuses a final offer must still pay the go-between.

The go-between arrived with the sellers. Everyone knows him; his friends number more than his heirs. He is the absolute authority, final arbiter, and disinterested judge. He makes no decisions yet causes all of them to be made. Hence he colors his cloak a bit gaudy and always buys the best cloth money can buy. He is the most astute judge of donkeys and donkey men in the region. Yet no one knows him except through his business dealings, for to reveal anything of himself would abdicate his detachment. Without that he would be out of business. So he dines quietly and alone, and in his rare nonbusiness conversations speaks of everything except donkeys and the knowledge they have given him. In the market he greets no one except any person coming to him and directly extending his hand, and he says nothing to anyone until he has heard both sides. He never, under any circumstances, adopts an expression that reveals his thoughts.

The buyer and his friends circle the donkeys, pausing little, their eyes casually noting everything. They miss nothing—every donkey limp, sore, chafed spot, dazed look, frothy mouth, bellow, belch, hoof, glassy eye, urine smell, spittle ball, belly, and tail. A followed female (one with still-nuzzling young) brings a higher price than a still-pregnant one, for a young donkey is a long-term investment but a newborn might not survive the rigors of a three-day trip to the next market, or the mother might fight with every other donkey in sight.

The friends of the buyer are the first to greet Guy's assistant as he tends the animal. These friends know within the first five or ten words whether the transaction is to be discussed further. From the age of the donkey they know roughly why it is being sold. From the dialect of Guy's assistant they know from where it came. From its place in the middle of the herd they know Guy is uncertain of the animal's worth. And from the direction of the gaze of the donkey's handler, they can guess which is Guy's group and perhaps can spot Guy himself.

Guy knows nothing except the defects of his donkey, and his rock-bottom conviction that he does not *have* to sell. A friend of Guy's, nearby but out of view, immediately detaches himself from whatever he has been doing and discreetly follows the buyer's contact man, who may or may not actually go directly to the buyer. The friend, if he is experienced, notes what kind of discussion follows. If it is long, he observes who does most of the talking and who does most of the listening.

The buyer's questions are conveyed by his agent back to the handler: how old and how much? The agent is the least senior in the transaction hierarchy, and so he counteroffers a price far lower than the buyer's. The buyer knows this, so the conversation is lighthearted. Quips and ripostes fly faster than marketsquare gossip. Meanwhile Guy and the real buyer are gauging one another's mettle amid the crowds of disinterested onlookers, passersby, friends, and tax agents. Eyes with airs of indifference reveal a buyer; ill-at-ease stares at the circle of donkeys unmask sellers.

The friends of each now converge and the air becomes thick with quotes of prices from sales long past. The donkey is tapped on the front knees with a stick, and it kneels on its haunches. How swiftly, how well, how ably it does so is remarked by everyone. Its teeth are examined, its age decided upon, its privates subjected to an undignified inspection, its virtues and docility solemnly pledged. The donkey kneels again, this time to find out how fast it rearises. Again it has its teeth and haunches inspected, for soft-flesh sores suppurate in unobvious ways.

At a handshake of agreement the donkey is led away by a young boy to the prospective buyer's own group of animals. Is it docile when led by a stranger? How does it amble? Does it bellow amid the others? Is it absorbed into them without snorts from them or foam from their mouths or kicks? The boy handler hasn't the authority to decide. Now dozens of others also are watching from the crowd, so that no one but the principals has a clear idea of who is speaking for whom. If the boy handler is the son of an important villager, his opinion is asked—but only after the sale.

As the donkey is led away the buyer signals to a trusted friend and they agree, knowing the price being asked, on what to seriously offer, what to aim for, and what to ridicule. Guy's demeanor is the most serious consideration—his strengths and weaknesses, the way he conceals in his words the knowledge revealed in his eyes. Perhaps Guy is a bit hard of hearing or cannot follow the pace of fast banter. Are his boasts a sham? How is he to be brought to reveal the true worth of his animal? The answers to these questions can change the price by a third or more.

Identical questions are being asked in Guy's camp and in both camps a strategy is advanced. The donkey is returned. Now buyer and Guy meet face to face for the first time. They speak first of the weather, the crops, their fields, the changing qualities of their sons, the inequities of tax collectors. Mutual acquaintances are invariably mentioned—the quality of their influence is invaluable. The buyer mentions his fine impression of the donkey; Guy congratulates him on his knowledge. The buyer tenders an offer, a respectable one, mentioning the lamentable necessity to point out a few drawbacks in this animal, and concludes with a shower of praises for Guy's obvious talent at donkey-keeping. Guy thanks the buyer profusely for his compliments, although they are far from deserved, but regrets that circumstances and the fine quality of his animal require that he accept no less than a sum about twice what the buyer has offered. If these two prices are respectable and fall into the range of each other's expectations, the sale concludes on a sliding scale which ends approximately halfway between the two.

But this does not always happen, so when either buyer or seller reaches a point of giving in no further, despite experience and logic, or if for some reason heated words are uttered, then at a mutual nod of the head, the go-between is summoned.

If the go-between has not been occupied with another transaction, like as not he already knows the dimensions of the drama from the length of the discussion. When he arrives he is informed straightaway who has offered what. His fee is based on a percentage of the difference between these two prices, with a required minimum just for the trouble of walking over. If either buyer or seller proves completely intransigent, the go-between is still entitled to a fee for his efforts.

He listens to Guy's case and his evaluation of the animal. Then Guy and his confidants, cousins, sons, and retainers move out of earshot. The same conversation ensues with the buyer. The go-between next makes a minute examination of the animal. He and he alone takes into consideration no judgment of either the buyer or Guy, but only that of the animal as animal.

Then a round of discussion. From buyer and Guy the go-between ascertains (as much from eyes as from words) the real buying and selling prices, the pride prices, and the insult prices. If the variance is too great, he tells them to call it a day. However, there is usually a respectable gap between the two, which he must bridge with words. Sometimes the bridge is a light, airy thing filled with webworks of nuance and fleeting references to family and heritage and fields plowed since long ago. Other times his words are a massive masonry of the most durable phrases he commands, chipped and polished slowly to an edifice of pure reason.

He cajoles, he pleads, he reminds them of exemplary donkeys bought and sold by their grandfathers. He states each one's case fairly and without sympathy to the other; they know it will be the same no matter who he represents. He points out, clarifies, spreads linguistic balm on wounded feelings. He never introduces a personal attitude, nor states his own mind, but he does state candidly what one or the other simply cannot accept, which he phrases "*can* not" accept. He exhorts both sides to keep trying, knowing that ill will ruins more sales than ill donkeys. He knows his profession exists solely because of pride's quirks when men who have money and men who need money meet face to face.

Eventually, amid the heat and gestures and exclamations and spitting into the dust, one price wavers and the other gains ground. The go-between now joins buyer to Guy, arm upon arm, until they shake hands. Immediately friends gather around and an enormous purse of coins is produced. The sum is counted and recounted, suspect coins replaced with others, to be counted again by both sides. The go-between leaves, for he builds ten or more of these bridges a day. He will be paid by everyone before they leave at dusk.

The difficult business done, the buyer and Guy separate—the buyer to do all the other buying he must do that day, and Guy and his friends to smile at the price they have exacted. They congratulate themselves, believe the congratulations of their friends, recount to their sons how much better the deal was than they had planned.

Now the subject of all these words is suddenly, almost incongruously, forgotten. In the quieting of the afternoon, as the sun slips from yellow on the horizon into an iridescent purple twilight, the donkey—which will transport flour and oil on the three-day trip back to the buyer's home, be reloaded with two large barrels of wine for a four-day journey to a market further on, and there be sold by the buyer for half again what he paid for it here—this animal, without which a centuries-old economy never would have begun, which every moment in its life has experienced nothing but orders, pokes, proddings, and toil (so like the lives of its owners under the Crown), this donkey now sidles up to its companions for the night, which signify their acceptance by smelling its urine.

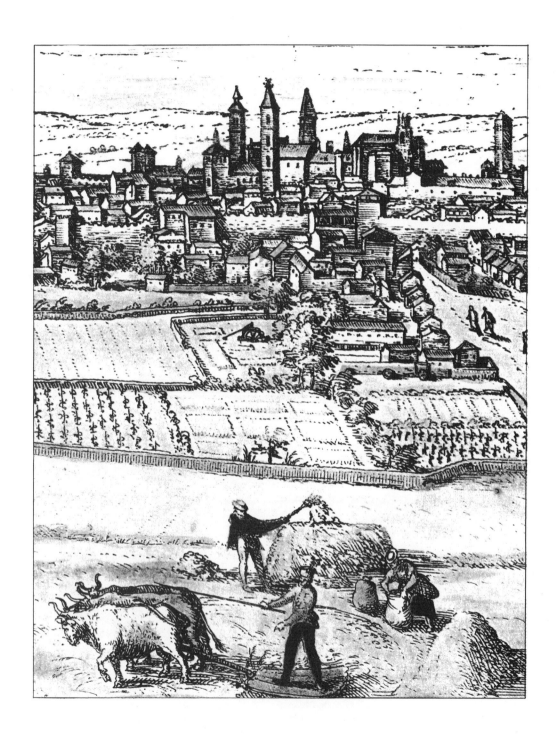

1669

—

Bread

Wheat achieves its perfection by being simple. Its stem has no need to branch. Its leaves are slender and tough and thrifty. It has eliminated petals, nectar, scent, color. It has no need of bees or butterflies. Soil and sun and water do everything.

And when it is wheat's time, its death is as simple as its life. The men come to the field with scythes, the women with sickles. The children carry baskets and woven reed pans. First they fetch water plants to weave into cords that will tie the sheaves. Hampers are hung over limbs, jackets over branches. Jokes about backaches begin the dry cycles of cut, bunch, sheave; cut, bunch, sheave.

The day heats so slowly that no one notices the sun until a jacket is taken off and lain in the stubble. Cut, bunch, sheave.

Then come the mules to bring in the cut wheat. It is bunched into sheaves spreading wide their gold crowns, tied onto the mules by strands of rough reed-work. At the threshing circle the children cut the knots and the bundles fall loosely into a pile. It is strewn into heaps while the men bring in the horses with broad hooves.

In the center of the circle there is a shaft on which a bar pivots, to which the horses are harnessed as they nicker belly-deep in dry stalks. Then, ears laid flat back, nostrils flaring for breath, they trudge in a circle until the husks of the grains are cracked under their hooves. Hour on hour, at the touch of the stick or the mumble of the drover, they continue their circling, smelling of sweat and leather and droppings and dust, endlessly merging hoofsteps into a dull circular world.

Finally the moment comes when they are released from the pole and led away to water and the streambank's fresh grass. The men and women then wade into the chaff. The men commence the *battage*, slamming down leather-bound flails to free the last grains from their husks. The women slide wooden spades into the heap and toss it up to the wind. The wind catches the flax and trails it into a cone far down the field. The spades rise and then throw, rise and then throw, with a pause in the middle to get the balance just right, rising and then throwing in a rhythm of pure motion.

Stopping only long enough to take water from a jar which was left unglazed and kilned at a low heat so the water would seep from inside and keep it cool. The women wear their skirts tucked up to their waists and bend low to scoop the grain into shallow leather baskets. Baskets scoop-shaped and broad, as wide around as their encircled arms, with reed handles for carrying the grain in the grain's time, the apples in apple time, lettuce and fruits, hay for the animals, dirt out of the house, fresh soil for the herbs, greens from the garden. And in the winter by the fire, they are lined with clean straw for the mother cat and her kittens.

The work is unpausing, backs aching from bending as they fill baskets and pouches with mounds of the grain. Four or five days for winnowing. Ceaseless hard work from the cold glow of dawn to the last light of dusk, and longer if there's a winnow moon, long hours that add up to a short life. And when they are finished, two-fifths must be sold to pay the King's tax, one-tenth must go to the *cure* of the church, another tenth is for the abbot and his clerks, and the rest . . . the rest can be kept. It takes a thousand years of history to make a peasant and thirty to kill him.

The road to the mill is a rutway ankle deep in fall mire. Like most roads it follows a creek. It was first broadened centuries ago by the prints of poets and pilgrims and priests, and now with the feet of merchants, tramps, tinkers, smiths, scholars. Prostitutes dressed as nuns, pedlars, Gypsies, friars. Then the ear hears the faint rumble and hiss of the mill, with its groaning wheel outside and clacking wooden gears inside changing the horizontal flow of a millrace's froth into the vertical spin of a stone. The ear senses the crushing grind of the stone's mass, as heavy as two barrels full of water and wider around than a plow-horse's belly.

Coming from the wet woods, where only the birds interrupt the mule's clops, the sound of the mill is a tumult of sonics and silence. Dozens of animals are tied up all around, for while the towns may boast of markets and fairs, the mill is the true countryman's place. No farmer would be so great a fool that this gathering of men should be only for words. And so with the baskets of wheat to be milled, perhaps a spare hen or ewe or rabbit can be sold . . . or won, for along the streambanks are circles where the grasses have been flattened into low stubs, trod now even lower as the harvest begins to come in. There, for longer than anyone can remember, they have arranged rock circles for their oldest of sports. Cockfights flurry in flashings of feathers, quick bets, cheers, dull croaks, hot blood mingling into the mud.

And here, too, the animals are shod, for the itinerant smith knows the mules of the mills like the lawyers know the estates with no heirs. The smith sets up early, clearing two pits as deep as his waist. Between them is his anvil. To his right the brazier, filled with charcoal made white hot by two leather bellows bound with wood hoops. To his left a bucket of water. Around him are his tongs, shears, pliers, hammers, lumps of crude metal, and a bucket of charcoal. He makes an adze blade quickly to order, pounding a lump of yellow-hot metal into a strip, flattening one end into a wide blade, then twisting the other into an oval loop for the handle. He bides his time between major projects by sipping on wine and pounding out nails. He takes a piece of bar as round as a finger and twice as long, hammers one end into a point, then flattens the other into a fan, which he curls with pliers into a loop. He throws it into the water, where it cools with a snapping sizzle.

Old friends salute and exchange their mild insults, mull over transactions, blacken the reputations of officialdom's wives, assess the merits of their children, and call upon God to bring justice to the tax farmer for the Crown.

NOT BY BREAD ALONE

For the tax comes each quarter, and in the ripeness of harvest does it seem the most wasted.

When the King and the Council decide on the tax, it has already been ten-tenthed on down to the bottom. They have been besieged by high nobles and ladies, who though they pay no tax of their own, also desire that their provinces be touched with a light bill. For that is where the revenues are drawn for their castles and carriages and tapestries and servants. The shift is to who is least able to mount trappings and pretense.

Every high official is similarly besieged. The wealthiest landowners pass their hour in the tapestry-lined rooms of official receptions. Speaking of their due as a thing of no consequence, bearing fine wines and warnings of doom, they smile in departure and salute their bowed grooms. Another lord's mistress redeems her pledge in the ancientest of ways, reaping the last fruits of a fading coquette.

In the least province the poorest district receives thus the main share, passing it on to the poorest back parish. After the *cure* has preached the first sermon and listed the week's lost sheep, the unwelcome news is read like a beckon from doom. "It's higher than ever!" "It's always been so!" The parish elders summon the council and it is agreed to have everyone come to the oak grove next to the church.

There are no good ways to raise bad money. All the men over twenty can vote as they choose, but only the elders do the talking. The first decision is the appointment of Collector. The argument seethes, for the Collector becomes the commune's most hated man for the rest of the year. From every throat there comes the cry of "Not me!" But once he's appointed he has to divide, and the assessment's size means his revenue can be neither simple nor graceful nor fair nor clean.

Last year's Collector of course will be generously rewarded, for he did his duty well and everyone nourishes a grudge. But then justice grows thinner. Must not the wealthiest farmers down in the village be let off with a light bill, for are not a dozen members of this meeting in debt to their loans? And someone's wife is almost high-born, her uncle's bought papers. So-and-so's brother is an official in the Dispensary of Salt; to assess him anything would be madness. The poorest village alone can be counted on to pay the whole of its tax.

The unfortunate Collector must now survive off whatever he can collect over his due. His face takes on the dutiful righteousness of the stone gargoyle on the church. He will be met by evasions and threats, passive resistance, expressionless shrugs. Payment comes in a sou at a time, often in the form of a plea to consider a spare hen as part payment, or a measure of butter plus a half-cheese. He tramps all over the region, his own fields neglected and falling to ruin, arguing, cajoling, bartering like a boy, finding himself the unwilling recipient of every unwanted odd and end in the village economy. Which somehow must be turned into gold livres before the year's end, or he is assured of a second year in tax-debtor's jail—a place from which one is ill-likely to emerge upright.

So the smallest prosperity is jealously whispered. Any fool living above subsistence can be sure his tax will be doubled next year. It becomes difficult to tell the bad farms from the good, families prefer their rags to their best, and who is so eager to shorten his life with the extra work of manuring his fields or bettering his stock only to lighten the burdens of an exasperated Collector? In the poorest places the villagers are happy with black bread and roots, with wine and cakes as autumn-end luxuries. Household gardens yield more than large fields, for they are by tradition invisible to the tax.

It is the peasant's duty to sweat and keep quiet, be submissive and serene, pray to fate and the luck of the weather, smile with approval at his petty lord's stories, say nothing of what he himself needs, mumble his words and not raise his voice, shrug off the inequities that gnaw at his life, and tack together as best he can the planks of a living. And when he dies all he owns goes to an insolent heir who strikes forlorn all his father's hopes that he had been blessed with a just son.

For this is a son not satisfied with bread alone. There is a new king. There is a new world far beyond the oceans. The roads are free of cutthroats for the first time in centuries. The world is open—for those who have plans.

All over the provinces these sons are well known: "One year he was Collector, the next year Sub-prefect" . . . "His good character was smashed in search of the dazzling." Through scant mercy and stern use of his powers, he maneuvers the ruin of an old family into a Master-of-Requests rank, the lowest rung on the courtier's ladder. And having bought a few coins' worth of hired history from an itinerant scribe, his sole shortcoming was wealth until an opportunity to administer Church funds works in one year a miracle.

He has moved his portrait out of the pantry into the anteroom, and his eye is on the salon. He is remorselessly modern, touches up his appearance with brushes and tints, piles onto subordinates more duties than they can handle, snaps at anyone whose demeanor is less certain, takes over more of a room than anyone else, corrects everyone in midsentence, indulges superiors' laughter but suppresses it in lackeys, speaks eloquently of the importance of assets and law, hints of his knowledge of statecraft and power, has assembled a stable and acquainted himself with the hunt, and gives to a passing beggar a coin of sly worth while exclaiming, "It is true what they say, an empty sack cannot stand."

Such are the times of the tolltaker's rise. The King is taken with palaces and knighthood. A court is content with intrigues and titles. In the legalist's hands a toll can be found for the drinking of water and walking on ground. Dressed in his new merits and scorning those old, he is to history a speck of dust hovering after a great army has passed.

Yet this is but a lappet in the mill's sea of glad talk. No one hurries for this is a family-and-field-free day they have to themselves. A grizzled relic with a mournful moustache rings in the laughter by rising and cackling, "I'm over eighty now, but who would believe it to see me in the fields tickling the titties and raking the hay?"

So the talk turns to fields. Fields they now own, fields they did own, fields they hope they will own, wish they might own, curse their luck for not having owned, or wouldn't own even if they could.

Only the soil can be trusted to bring forth its full. The peasant lives between that soil and his hut. He plows it in March, rakes and harrows it in April, sows wheat in it in May, eats the bread which lays all day upon it in June, drinks it in the dark water he scoops up with his hands in July, spits it as it swirls from behind his scythe in August, rises to see it as it looms out of the first light, slumbers on it in the heat of midday, dreams about it as he thinks of his sons, curses it as it vanishes away with the wind, knows his worth by it and that of his neighbors, and when he knows he will soon rest in it wracks his brain how fairly to divide it. He does not think in the same way of any other thing, even heaven.

Beneath the sound of speaking men is the streaming of living water, first heard against the fishing weirs and boats, then against the mill's tamped dam, then through a sluice into the millrace, then jetting against the great wheel. Some of the paddles are missing so the wheel's turn is a slow cycle from the groan at the bottom's struggle to the shriek at the top's fall.

The millhouse is built of rough stone and oak timbers, boat-shaped to part the water uneddyingly and join it again, with a shingled roof and maze of sheds. A dozen years of autumn leaves have clogged its gutters. Flour dust fans out from cracks and mouse holes. The men working inside cough and spit white, and everyone shouts against the stone's hollow roar.

The stone's granite faces are a flinger of flour that takes an hour to work through a man's load. Above them is a bin with a trough that leads out over a hole in the top stone's center. A stick wedged into the trough adjusts the wheat's flow. Men pour their sacks of grain into the bin. It trickles slowly into the spinning maw of the stone and vanishes almost instantly to dust, to be swept up by a whisk and scooped into sacks, so fine and pure it brings a lump to a man's throat.

Theodule Lefief left home with five sacks of grain before dawn and now returns before supper minus the twentieth taken as a toll, with the pullet no one wanted for dinner, a few nails, a wine flush on his cheeks, gossip enough for a week, and the smile of a day among friends.

The town ahead awakens and stretches itself after the afternoon nap. "Get Up!" calls bring kids into the streets, boys to the woodpiles, girls to the wellheads. Chores, hunger, cats chased out, cows up to the pastures, bacon frying, gossip telling, dinner planning . . .

Bread baking.

Inside a dark door, next to a smoking chimney, Theodule's wife Brun, a heavy woman whose short hair has the lusterless look of a lifetime without having

NOT BY BREAD ALONE

been washed, stirs her oven's coals. The chimney erupts into smoke as twigs catch into the embers. Then she brings out the pans where she'll make the dough.

Thick-waisted farm wives get there by way of their backs, becoming barrel-stave strong and almost as bent. Then they are ready to bear their ten or more children, of whom a few will survive to become as strong as themselves. They acquire first the nimblenesses of kneading and knitting, then the skill of milking the cow, then breeding (first the animals and later themselves), and finally ending life working harder, relaxing less, and dying sooner than their men.

Clad in a dull black frock, Brun wrings her work-warped hard hands as she inspects the new flour to see if it contains one of the miller's tricks, a layer of acorn or barley flour slipped in during sacking. She has never heard the troubadour's smooth lines about women stealing men's speech by giving them sighs. Her day is apportioned to the thousand small things that make up a meal.

The warmth of her life is the stone of the hearth, place of a thousand snapped cinders and a thousand late meals. At the edge of the fire is a black iron kettle, flat-bottomed and fat, the treasure of her dowry. It is set well back on the stones, where the heat is the deepest. Heat so long replenished by each day's new wood that the hearth hasn't cooled since the day she was wed.

Her bed is of fern on a floor of tamped dirt, where the night is of loomings from embers flicking a blue light. Yet everything is immaculate, for her home is of shelves and household things, bound twigs and feather whisks, pottery jars for soap-making, sweet oils and scents of flowers and salt, herb jars, laurel and lemon, candles, medallions of saints, and a rosary of strung beans.

For the magics of the soul are not for the mind's touch. A flight of twilight birds smoothing a pond into calm silver are the gray ghosts of the water sky, the looming bands of Satans coming to swirl for a soul. The night squalls of starlings in search of a tree are witches come to take away the young calf. The devastation of thunderstorms is avenged by the lacework of swallows, always flying after them in loops. An itinerant pedlar tells of a night in the deep woods, of seeing a fire with dancing around. Was it witches at a sabbat, or woodcutters feasting with wenches?

Witchwork is of night beings inflamed by a half-light's truth. Brun crosses herself to ward off bad spirits as she opens the bag of flour.

For bread is not in man's but in God's hands. Hero wheat shares no lime-light. Falsetto yeast sings only on days of wet warmth. Eggs and rubbed salt are content with small parts. The hands weave all these into the shape of a loaf. But what is it, the thin spirit of all things, that makes bread rise?

First water and blossoms are put into jars stoppered with green twigs. Out in the sun Brun spreads a damp cloth on top of a wood board. Her ring and her breadboard were the first givings of her man. Off to the side she wets a glazed bowl. Then on a quern, a little hand mill, she crushes some walnut shells. She kneels with her skirt tucked up to her knees, and conjures bread from powders and sprinklings and a hand's obedience to a hummed tune.

Into the bowl go a dozen handfuls of flour, then water, eggs, and dark crystals of salt. Furrows of beads blend into the dust. Next she bends and starts kneading with her fists. It's the first motion she can remember her mother teaching her. Folding and turning, then rolling the soft ball, she watches it begin to wrinkle and glaze, and finally toughen to hold a thumb's dent.

She takes care of her hands, for they are the windows onto the invisible world.

The thumbs are Satan's, his handles on your soul. Of the two, the left one is the worst. If that thumb is taken from a body less than nine days dead, it becomes the Lamp of the Burglars, keeping victims asleep no matter how loud the noise. And if the body is that of a child, the thumb can cure any other child's warts.

But in God's universe all truths are opposite. The next finger to the thumb, the one most often used, is the body's conduit to God. A single drop of its blood, if lost onto the earth, will be seized by underground spirits in slake of their thirst: you must beware dying by water. Yet the same blood softened in water is a cure for bad humor.

The middle finger is Doom, the finger of death. He who dies lacking Doom must wander forever, never finding peace in the Being Without End. But if at the death of one who is so lacking a carved wooden finger is placed in its stead, the soul can be claimed by the Devil or by God, whomsoever possessed the first right. Three drops of its blood, if touched to a willow stick, will enable the holder to know where a lost thing is to be found.

The fourth finger is the body's own, its aperture to life. With it medicines must be mixed, and measurements are made in relation to its volume and length. If a red yarn is tied to it in a coil or spiral, one who has a fever will fling off the bad choler.

And the little finger is Margot, the Magpie, the wing of the thumb that is the harbinger of death. If it is the thief of the soul, is it not also the best thief of men's things? When it touches an object covetously, there is no need for a purse, for the thing will vanish to wherever you like, with Satan there waiting and holding the bill.

Brun twists her fingers amid the knowledge of these truths, smiling at her mysteries and the aloneness of wisdom. Only if all the fingers are used, each doing as much as it must, only then will the bread rise.

And they do, losing their pink sheen. She kneads the loaf again, this time softening her fists. Too much of her weight will make a crust that's too coarse, and too little of it will make the loaf coarse within.

One handful is spun rounded and flat, another rolled into a long twist. She coats them on the bottom with the walnut dust so they won't stick to the hearth, then covers them with a cloth and puts them aside.

So now her bread can rise as fine as it may, while she thinks of supper. A jubilant supper! For isn't it autumn and the harvest was good? Isn't it Monday the Day of Jubilation? Sunday is past. Christ has delivered mankind again by the bread of his life. Tomorrow the week can begin its long descent to Friday, Day of Death, day of Christ's passion, when bread becomes flesh and wine becomes blood.

So a fine supper! What's it to be? Ah! Pocket soup and mortrew, and for a treat, meat cooked in almonds and garlic, with sorrel and tarragon strained in with its juice. And for a sweet, strained grape pulp mixed with honey and cream.

Pocket soup she makes when there is fat meat. Trimmings and trotters are splintered on stones, then simmered in herb water until the water is near gone. Then it is cooled until it jells almost as firm as lean, and rolled into a pouch lined with sweet gums and celery leaf. To make soup, she slices it into boiling water and sprinkles it with an aroma made of powdered flowers and thyme.

She thinks a mortrew of chicken and fish. White meats are boiled then mortared to paste. This is mixed with bread crumbs and egg yolks, shaken in a gourd until it froths, and boiled again until the mass congeals. She'll serve it with diced bacon and pieces of smoked tongue on a trencher of hard bread.

These things are half done when the bread is fully risen. What has puffed it up if not the spirit of the Being? Behind the stone house is a brick dome with a fire pit and a stone door. The smoke of its fire is dwindling and the coals are bright red.

Brun now works swiftly, turning out the loaves onto a flat board, rubbing them with water and quickly slicing crosses on top so bad spirits won't spoil the bake—so quickly she misjudges and gives herself a slight cut! She looks at it gravely and swiftly tells the oven her secrets to ward off bad spirits. Then in go the loaves, sliding to a rest on the hot stones. She takes out the plank and puts in a small bowl of water. It slides to the center, where the heat is the fiercest, and begins to sizzle and steam. Then she crosses herself three times.

Three, the magic number of God.

Three persons in the Trinity. Three persons in Christ's family. Three epochs of history: creation, present, hereafter. Three ends of being: heaven, hell, and limbo. Three arts of the trivium: grammar, rhetoric, and dialectic. Three ages in the life of man: learning, experience, knowledge. Three estates of society: priest, noble, peasant.

Yet three multipled of itself is more magical still. Heaven has nine choirs of angels, the Church has nine hierarchies, a prayer said thrice times thrice has the power of nine times nine.

Yet if three is the number of God, four is the number of Earth: the four winds, the four directions, the four elements of air, earth, fire, and water; the four points of Christ's cross; the four points of the compass; the four paradisical rivers of Matthew, Mark, Luke, and John; the four cardinal virtues; the four bodily humors; and the four sciences of the quadrivium: geometry, arithmetic, astronomy, music.

Yet these create but harmonies, they are not music. Only when summed do they become the most mystical hymn of nature, seven: seven planets, seven virtues, seven deadly sins, seven sacraments, seven notes in the Church's chant, seven ages of man, seven seals in Revelation, seven directions in Heaven's unity of thought: thing, mind, matter, past, present, future, God.

Only when wheat rises does it become bread.

Life rich in this needs no physical perfection. Bent from a poor birth and crushed life, the wonder is why it isn't the weather or work that abrades, but the tiny cut on a finger. The scratch from a rough place on a piece of wood. A too-serious disagreement with the cat. A swift cut from a blade that nicks too far into the edge of a loaf. A scratch that can swell, become blue, spread swiftly for no reason. Brun licks at the cut, sees it's on Magpie, and doesn't like that sign.

She goes to her votive place, her small shelf with candles and amulets and an image of the Virgin once blessed by a priest. She bows her head and prays, "Three biters go away, three betters help me today." Saying this three times, she takes off her ring and kneels for a Hail Mary.

Three biters: cuts, pricks, abrasions. Three ways the blood can be cursed. Three paths for the soul's escape.

Three betters: Father, Son, Spirit—the trinity of One that listens to a prayer.

She shakes her finger to make sure the bleeding has stopped, then returns to the bread. The stone door falls away at the pry of her stick. She bakes the bread to color, letting it take its own time. Then the loaves are ready and she scoops them out with a board. They crackle fiercely when they first meet the cool air, thick-crusted and light brown, sending out an aroma that'll soon have neighborhood kids clamoring for a piece.

She looks at her hand, meeting place of magic and wheat. If a swallow's flight can chase away a huge storm, and a year can begin dying from the same rain that once brought it life, and the dance of a pond's colors can reveal the beings beneath, then what is bread?

She prays from the last pews of the church, for to approach God directly means to be naked before every eye of the universe. But a saint can be prayed to from even a poor hearth. The world is of men and magic, but it's bread that's the miracle.

1788

Pilloried

He is pilloried sitting down, legs and arms clenched in two boards' hold, splattered by street boys with overripe tomatoes, spoiled cabbages, eggs that had long been left in the sun. Taunted by youths, yelled at by workmen, smirked at by the coiffed wives of merchants. Three days thus in the sun, the rain, the cold, the wind. Water and hard bread brought once each morning, fetid soup at night. Hungry, sitting in his own excrement, head resting on the gnawing edges of the boards, half-dead with stiffness, he cries out for mercy and hears only the words, "By the Grace and Beneficence of the Crown shall Sylvain Lefief be pilloried for the crime of stealing bread."

The pillory was placed in the square next to the market cross, many centuries after it. Where men once believed in the pledge of their word, where twice made custom and custom made law, where a simple oath over clasped hands in front of the cross pledged a man's word against his salvation, now was the pillory. The market of old had become merchants and moneychangers and lawyers and taxmen, men who knew a law they could make for themselves was a cup that never lacked liquor.

Hardly has the bailiff finished closing the pillory's headboard over Sylvain's neck with the sound of a dull wooden *chunk* when the town's boys gather to break in this new criminal. The rottenest of old eggs are hurled against his head—fetid, foul, sulfurous, reeking more than the combined chamber pots of hell. Then comes the spit, the rotten fruit, the spoiled milk, the vinegary remnants from the bottoms of barrels. Within two hours the stench's fumes rise in waves.

Then comes a time of quiet as the market lunches. Sylvain bows his head and cries, pouring out hopelessness, with broken-shouldered sobbing, feeling the humiliation of injustice. But when the sharpness of tears is done there remains not remorse but the raw, long, lingering heat of hatred, fury worsened by a helplessness unable even to shoo away the stinging clouds of flies and wasps and mosquitoes. The flies soon learn that the trembling of a pinioned arm is the worst they have to fear, and the mosquitoes are too stupid to care. Stench, slaps, the stupid smug stares of stupid stupid people with stupid stupid faces, the ache beyond relief, the intolerance of a town that has progressed from sin to crime, from God to bread.

No intolerance is too great for the man who cannot buy his loaf. Three hours at the pillory would be enough, nobody would ever forget it. But three days?

On the third day, after he washed himself in the river, Sylvain Lefief beats a petty lord to death with a broken-off limb so he can take the man's knife, and finds himself three years later cheering himself hoarse as the guillotine slides down its trunnion to come to rest with the sound of a dull wooden *chunk*.

1788: PILLORIED

1889

Chemin de Fer

A hundred years ago the hardest metal France knew was made for the guillotine. Now an even harder metal, steel, wraps all France in silvery ribbons, and on them pass the *chemin de fer*.

Gerard has already been walking an hour and a half. For the first time now he can see the light of day as he nears Port Boulet.

It is a two-hour route he has often walked before. Past Le Pressoir, an oak-arbored hollow near the three farmhouses of Le Peu Muleau, where during the grape harvest an itinerant pressman blocks up the wheels of a cart with a wine press bolted to it, lets his donkeys loose in the meadow of Guillotiere nearby, and waits for the local farmers to bring the harvest from their household arbors and the few rows of unkempt vines bordering their gardens.

Past Les Caves Saint Martin, where time out of mind ago local farmers had hollowed caves while cutting the soft stone to build their houses and fences, which caves they now use to store their *futs* and *cercles* of wine to age through winter.

Past Le Moulin, the long disused mill on the banks of the little stream Lane, a mill made obsolete by manufactured flour brought by the chemin de fer from La Beauce, the great granary of France embracing Chartres cathedral with kilometer upon kilometer of wheat.

Past Les Mellieres, a damp meander locked in the embrace of the Lane, where once the herb gatherers came to pick nettle which when boiled was said to calm the pain of women in their flow; now it is a thicket of tall plants no longer picked because no one remembers how to prepare the balm.

Past Forgier a hundred steps beyond, a hamlet so ancient that only the oldest men in the village can recall it was named for the descendants of a smith who had once set up his forge there. So few now remember the family that even the name of their place is fading.

Past Huberdelliere, at one time said to be the finest pasture for kilometers around, now being inexoribly filled with sand and river debris by the owners of the gravel quarry along the Loire nearby, whose lawyer reasons that as no one now keeps pasturage there it de facto has been abandoned, and therefore he who makes use of it should have it for that use. Local people have already begun to call it Gravellois.

Gerard looks to his right toward the stone abbey of Bourgueil, now scarcely more than a pile of stones amid broken walls and an arcade of unbroken arches, the friars of which were expelled by rioting villagers during the Revolution.

With a kilometer still to go Gerard begins to scent the astringent metallic oil-and-steel smell of the rails and ties of the chemin de fer. Then he reaches Port Boulet's short stretch of gravel-and-oil road. The coal merchant's shutters are not yet open, which relieves Gerard, for his parents owe the man forty francs and the merchant never ceases to harangue Gerard every time he passes. Marcel, the waiter in the best of the town's two cafes—famed locally for its specialty of lark patties simmered in the white wine of Saumur—is polishing the brass door handle with the sleeve of his shirt. Gerard takes an alley to bypass Marcel, for he doesn't want to have to explain that he is leaving the family home for good, that he wants to be the first of the Lefiefs to make his way to success in the grandest city in the world.

At eighteen, Gerard has prepared for Paris. He read a newspaper printed in Paris once, after he had worked two days to earn the sou that was its price. He had walked the nine kilometers from the family home at Haute Champ to the station of the chemin de fer at Port Boulet simply for the privilege of obtaining a newspaper there. And while reading of Paris—the fashions, the politics, the business affairs, the mistresses, the cartoons—he watched the engines steam in, the people embark, and knew that one day he would be one with them.

Today is that day. As he takes the back road around La Jacqueliniere to the station, he counts the eleven francs in his pocket that have taken him three years to earn. He passes vegetable sellers, two old men and a woman, pushing their barrows along, their heads bowed low as they lean into their loads.

Gerard shakes his head in relief: Paris will never have such sights! He reads the *Journal de la Jeunesse*, and there are no pictures of barrow pushers there! The *Journal*'s engravings portray a clean, bustling Paris with crowds of polite, well-dressed people making their way in *fiacres* or promenading along paved streets with monuments on every corner, all freshly cleaned by the rains.

He reaches the station half an hour after dawn and, for the twentieth time that year, examines the schedules. There will be a train to Orleans at 7:15 and another to Paris at 7:45.

The chemin de fer even has pictures of itself. The poster of the express train "Cote d'Azur" on the billet-window wall shows a squat, proud engine speeding into an orange-colored sunset, blurring the wagons-lits trailing behind amid stream-lines of smoke from the engine's steam valves and exhaust chimney. The picture of the dining car shows the cook in a white smock, separated from the flower-adorned white tables by a low partition so the diners can see him work. Vines grow from polished brass pots embraced in the stylish curves of metal brackets. On the white-clothed tables are vases filled with flowers the poster says are cut every morning in Angers.

The officials of the chemin de fer wear new uniforms, for this being the year of the centennial of the Revolution all France is garbing itself in garments of white. A week from today will be July 14. Gerard will stand with the multitude in the Place de la Bastille as the fusiliers stand to attention holding their historic weapons and the politicians stand on bunting-draped platforms with their wives or mistresses, and children will cry and put their hands over their ears as great cannons thunder and fill the Place with flint-smelling smoke.

121

Gerard goes onto the platform, a length of cord-du-roy logs whose tops had been planed to a flat surface, then set side by side. Weeds grow from the crevices and knotholes. On some spur tracks nearby a team of oxen whose yoke has been moved up to their foreheads push on gondola cars to shunt them under a gravel chute, where they will be filled with small stones from nearby Gravellois. Men come up to the station bookstall, throw down a sou, snatch a copy of the *Mercure de France* or *Figaro*, find seats in the waiting room and read, oblivious to anything but the news.

Here Gerard sees his first *citoyen*. He must be a *citoyen*–a citizen of Paris–Gerard reflects, for he is dressed in a light grey tweed suit with black edging around the collar and sleeves and pocket flaps, a white collar, a striped cravat, a black bowler hat with a velvet band, and black leather shoes. He is totally unlike the others on the platform, with their durable country clothes of serge in dark colors. Not a woman on the platform could compare with him! The man examines the others with an air of disdain. He carries a malacca walking stick with a gold head, which he stamps on the cord-du-roy every few moments to indicate his displeasure at the time consumed awaiting the chemin de fer. Gerard stares at the man. He half expects the man to speak French with a British accent, for such is the cut of his clothes. Later Gerard learns that many well-to-do men of the provinces wear the British style when they ride the chemin de fer, presuming the railcar to be a form of boulevard in which it is perfectly appropriate to ape the dandies of the *boulevards de Paris de grand luxe.*

As to what he will do for subsistence when he arrives in Paris, Gerard does not know. When his father is not picking apples or gathering grapes in seasonal labor, he carries bricks and timber in the building trade. Gerard knows the language of that trade, so surely he can be of use there. He will do that until an opportunity presents itself–and of course it will, for is it not Paris?

The chemin de fer is half an hour late. The dandy has tired of stamping his cane and has retired to the bookstall to peruse with tepid interest a copy of the cahiers of the local historical society, in which several authorities from Chinon identify all the places near Bourgueil mentioned in the great chronicles of Rabelais. At the mere thought the dandy rolls his eyes.

122

Gerard secretly gazes at the man, then goes into the W.C. and looks himself up and down in the mirror. There is nothing he can do about the black serge suit and black shoes, but at least he can get rid of the antiquated starched collar, so he throws it on the floor. Then he hears the engine coming and walks quickly to the far end of the platform and puts himself out of sight behind an oak tree.

The engine driver sees Gerard hiding and the rattan valise he is carrying and knows what Gerard is up to, so he shouts "Bon courage!" as he passes. He stops the engine so the vestibule of the very last wagon is directly in front of Gerard. The *chef de gare* is at the other end of the platform repeating, "Vos billets, monsieurs et mesdames, vos billets!" There is no other ticket taker in sight. Gerard passes behind the wagon to the other side of the train and runs up the steps. A whistle screeches, the train shudders, and he is on his way to Paris!

In an increasing blur of speed, past Lavoir and Sechoir, where the washerwomen come down to the water wearing the signs of their trade, cloth strips knotted around their knees. Past Pic-Vert, where the green woodpeckers store acorns in fall and retrieve them in spring. Past Sanglier, where the boar hunters come to sell their meat. Then past names he no longer knows – Armeaux, Bourgosiere, Goulieres, Loges, Bouchardiere, Poitiviniere, Noyers. Past Avoine, where the chateau of Usse looms in the distance, past Cinq-Mars-la-Pile, past Forneau, past Fontenay – name after name after name until Gerard finally sleeps.

When Gerard awakens he has forgotten the names forever, even the name of his family. In Paris he will be no Lefief, he will be Jacques Lutece and he will be what he makes of himself. Beyond the windows of the wagon looms the great girdered tower of Monsieur Eiffel, completed hardly three months before, now proud with a *tricolour* at its top flowing in a thin breeze. The countryside has slipped into the past as quickly as the chemin de fer races into Paris. The countryside becomes houses and houses become apartments and apartments become metropolis as the silver rails speed into the city. Paris! Oh! The speed of it! Oh, the beautiful speed of it! The speed! The speed! The City! The City!

1989

The Last Remains of the Family Lefief

S he stares out from an old photo, uneasy at sitting still and being the center of attention, in a shapeless wool dress with one hand holding a Bible and the other draped over a carved wooden table. The photographer told her to look into the camera, and that she dutifully did, unsmiling and unblinking, getting on in years as the shutter was snapped, her puffy thick fingers and soiled cuticles revealing a lifetime of cows and cooking and cold water, in this the only portrait of her life.

Her husband's photo has the same pose minus the Bible. Faded pencil on the back of his picture reads: "1905, To Marie-Claire from Jacques."

Good, solid, uneventful countryside names, as plain and hardworking as their shoes. Not the French of Matisse and chateaux and musicians and world trade, but of gardens and furrows and drudgework and rain, lived in a poverty affording but one portrait in a lifetime—and that with a borrowed bow tie and white lace caplet. Lives not of comforts or goods or openings at theatre, but of the sun and the wind and the dusk and the summer, the indomitable peasant spirit, and the immense span of centuries that was their being.

Their goods must not have been great, for in 1905 one visited the photographer wearing one's best. And there are no children in the pictures, although the Lefiefs are neither too young nor too old and it was the custom of the time to be photographed as family. They probably didn't have any, which would have

125

been poverty redoubled in a time when five or more children were needed to take care of a farm's tasks each day.

And when they died, what was left? The photographer has long since passed out of business, so there's no trace of them there. The name Lefief is as common as Jones, so there's no use searching the records in old churches. A table, a few chairs, a plow, rakes, hoes, two or three changes of clothing, some debts left unanswered, a cow or two, some chickens, and the two photographs.

World War I would have taken care of the chickens and cows: Troops passed through eating whatever they could. The debts died of their own accord. The furniture might have gone to neighbors or relatives, but after World War I the French were so eager to modernize that rustic and not particularly well-built furniture went quickly into wintertime fireplaces. Years later a newly acquired taste for such things led to their being cleaned up and sold for astronomical prices—money that would have cleared the Lefiefs of all debts and left a subsistence besides.

The rakes, hoes, and plows would have lasted longer, the need for such things in the countryside being eternal. But there are only so many repairs that can be made and one by one they would have been stacked in some unused corner of a shed, forgotten until the shed should be torn down. The clothes would have been worn nearly to ruin by whoever inherited them, then cut into quilting, and when the quilt went it would have been cut into rags, and when the rags went they would have gone into the fire.

The photographs would have gone to the family member interested in genealogy and keeping the family records. And when all had been duly noted and the scrapbook put back on the shelf, the Lefiefs would have been forgotten except at baptisms and weddings. Although the scrapbook survived World War II, its owner probably did not, perhaps passing on during Hunger Winter in 1944, when people were boiling and eating rats.

Now, three generations later with the economic boom of the sixties giving the French their first real taste of prosperity since the 1800s, anything with memories of the old days is thrown out to make room for new houses, new furniture, new cars.

The scrapbook found its way to a flea market in Bourgueil, where it was disassembled by a stallholder into the fantasy postcards, the historical-scene post-cards, the touristic postcards, the handwritten genealogies, a few envelopes with saleable stamps, and these two photographs.

The postcards were bulked out to a dealer from Holland, the empty scrap-book sold to a collector, the genealogies trashed, and the photographs laid out on the ground alongside some pieces of pipe from a plumber, a hubcap, three screwdrivers, a wool scarf, and a couple of dolls.

The day started off with everything priced at a franc. Toward four in the afternoon everything dropped to half a franc, and by half past four everything was a *vingtieme*, a twenty centime coin worth about five cents. Someone stepped on the photos, breaking them in half. Ten minutes before the market closed, they were down to ten centimes.

At five minutes before five, when the remnants of the market day would be tossed to the trash, I came along and with a little haggling got the last remains of the Family Lefief for a five-centime piece. But for a penny they would have been lost.